The Addicted Child

The Addicted Child

a parent's guide to navigating the crisis, and chaos of a child's substance use disorder

DAVE COOKE

Founder of 100Pedals

THE ADDICTED CHILD
A PARENT'S GUIDE TO NAVIGATING THE CRISIS, AND CHAOS OF A CHILD'S SUBSTANCE USE DISORDER

iUniverse books may be ordered through booksellers or by contacting:

iUniverse
1663 Liberty Drive
Bloomington, IN 47403
www.iuniverse.com
1-800-Authors (1-800-288-4677)

Because of the dynamic nature of the Internet, any web addresses or links contained in this book may have changed since publication and may no longer be valid. The views expressed in this work are solely those of the author and do not necessarily reflect the views of the publisher, and the publisher hereby disclaims any responsibility for them.

Any people depicted in stock imagery provided by Getty Images are models, and such images are being used for illustrative purposes only.
Certain stock imagery © Getty Images.

ISBN: 978-1-5320-5641-3 (sc)
ISBN: 978-1-5320-5642-0 (e)

Print information available on the last page.

iUniverse rev. date: 08/22/2018

Get in touch:

Dave Cooke: www.100pedals.com

Media requests and special/bulk orders: graftonandscratch@gmail.com

I wanted to take a few minutes now while it's fresh in my mind to let you know just how poignant this book has been for me. I've had so many "ah-ha" moments and so much of what you've addressed rings true in my experiences. It is a MUST READ for any parent whose child has an addiction. It's a great parenting book in general as well. I wish I had it 16 years ago. – Brenda Ferdland

I found all the information very valuable to my life's road. The way you write is very relatable, which made your points easy for me to understand. – Kim Grimes

You touched on everything that I feel with my own daughter's journey and some parts left me breathless. Like "HE GETS IT!!" This will benefit so many families! If they are ready to create real change, this will be one of the major tools that can help them succeed. – Katie Donovan

Introduction

Protecting our kids from harmful influences, including those who would promote the use of narcotics, is something all parents hope to accomplish. Unfortunately we cannot insulate our children from the predatory forces active in their schools and communities, nor can we adequately patrol all aspects of their lives or perfectly manage who they choose as friends or liaisons.

Our children are of their own world and unfortunately some of them will make poor lifestyle choices. Some adolescents and young adults will fall prey to the harmful and self-serving influences of certain individuals they encounter.

We simply cannot hold our children or grand-children close enough to protect them from everything they may face in their young lives.

As a result, some young people will become involved in using substances that pose great harm, or perhaps will be recruited into the drug trade itself - even from as early as elementary school age. Sadly, some of our wonderful, vulnerable young people will fall down, facing years struggling to gain back all that has been taken from them during their time battling an addiction.

Taking a strong prevention position against the under-age use of drugs or alcohol has proven to be a positive influence on dissuading youth use, however education alone does not *Teflon* them or offer a guarantee of abstinence. Nothing insures their sobriety, even a concerned parent's best efforts.

The Addicted Child is a book which addresses the harsh road a parent faces when confronted with a child's drug use and subsequent addiction.

Dave Cooke, as the father of a son who became addicted to heroin, has walked the walk and now talks the talk of a parent faced with the devastating crisis brought upon his youngest child.

Pamela McColl – child rights activist and author: *The Pied Pipers of Pot, On Marijuana – a powerful examination of what marijuana means to our families and communities, Baby and Me Tobacco Free,* and an award winning edition of a smoke-free *Twas The Night Before Christmas – edited by Santa Claus.*

Mile 1

A harsh reality, the news of a child's addiction.

We are hard-wired to take care of our kids and to make sure that they have their teeth brushed, their shoes on, their homework done, that they get to their part-time job on time, they treat people with respect, are safe from illicit drugs, bullying, violence and other harms prevalent in our society.

There are a lot of things we do to influence, even control our children. When they are toddlers, we can pretty much demand they follow the rules. Even then, they often still make their own decisions. When they are young children, they are most likely to go along with our recommendations and rules.

With the onset of adolescence, the relationship changes and our children become more concerned about fitting in with their peers and belonging to a particular social group, including those who may have very different views on appropriate behavior and societal norms than their parents. As our children grow older it becomes more difficult to get them to do the things that we want them to do.

One thing is for certain, as our children get older, we as parents can influence and encourage, but we cannot control.

Nothing brings a harsher reality to this statement than parenting a child who is using drugs or has substance use disorder. When it comes to substance use disorder, our children are fighting a life and death battle. As parents, we soon discover that, despite our best efforts, we are unable to directly chart their course to a successful recovery.

The situation hits hardest, and hurts most, when we come to the realization we really have no control over the direction their drug use will take them. Our inability to fix the problem, change the circumstances, or make this nightmare end is painfully frustrating and can be utterly exhausting. After all, we have always been able to take care of our children, until now.

It is a harsh reality to discover we can do little to help them or control them. Acknowledging this reality is the first step or mile in this parenting battle.

The next challenge comes with getting on with our lives in face of this reality. Accepting the present situation requires a major adjustment. This is where I have watched many parents struggle. Instead of adjusting their life in the face of the realization their child is involved in drugs, they continue to fight to create a different reality. They become embroiled in saving, protecting, or controlling a child in the face of their addiction struggle, only to painfully discover defeat time and again.

Deciphering what is within or beyond your direct control is paramount in moving forward and not being stuck in a battle of wills that cannot be won. We can only control that which is ours to control.

A child's addiction driven choices are not in our control. You may indirectly influence their behavior, but if you expect your will, your power, your love or your desire to control to be effective, you are setting yourself up for disappointment and failure. Yes, the expression of love is powerful and reminding your child they are loved is a wonderful parental gift. But outright attempts to control them, even from a place of love will likely fail. Substance use disorder is a personal crisis, it's your child's battle, and it rests solely within their control and their self determination to seek help, follow through, to do the work and to succeed.

You can love them unconditionally and meet them where they are with a message of hope and encouragement. The rest is up to them.

What you can control is how you live, how you choose to do to move forward with the life you have, and how you choose to respond to this crisis in your own life. You have the ability to find peace in the moment, to take comfort that nothing lasts forever, with time things do change, situations can improve, and there will be another mile on the road ahead.

Celebrate those opportunities to change, improve, and appreciate your life. It is most productive to focus on living the life you have and stop fighting to control the life you fear you have lost. When you do this, you will find peace!

Here is the story of my fight to reclaim my life, as the father of an addicted child.

Mile 2

By way of a phone call, I received the news that my youngest son, who at the time was 20 years old, had been arrested.

This news blew me away! I never saw this coming. Imagine getting a phone call that your son's in jail! What?! Wait a minute, jail?! What did he do? How did it happen? I collected myself, hung up the phone and I told my wife what was going on as best I could.

Shortly thereafter we received a follow-up phone call from our daughter who was able to explain in detail the circumstances of the arrest. As it turned out my son had become addicted to heroin, was homeless and had been arrested for a theft necessitated by his addiction. I remember thinking, how could this be my kid who is under arrest? It just didn't make any sense.

There are so many things I had dreamt or envisioned for my son's future. This clearly wasn't one of them. Instead, my wife and I were facing the unbelievable scenario that our son's life had completely fallen apart.

We were both shattered by the news. Disbelief and sadness were the definitive emotions of the day.

I hit the panic button. I reacted and started doing what I thought to be the best course of action at the time.

I went into rescue mode.

What can I do to fix this? How can I help? I bought a plane ticket and travelled to where my son was living, determined to gather him up and bring him closer to family, where a change of venue and a parents' love would be all he needed to move past this mess.

Surprisingly, my son wanted nothing to do with moving to where we were living. He wanted to remain in his hometown, he didn't want to relocate to a new city. I was his dad, I was on a mission, I knew what was best, and my son not coming with me was not an option. Despite his objections I transplanted him.

Over the next two years, we went through a cycle of very painful episodes involving theft, deception, arrests, jail, relapses, and near-overdoses. Time after time something would derail my well laid out plans to get him back on track. Every time something went terribly wrong it felt like we were losing ground and losing our son.

With every adverse event I became increasingly obsessed over my failings as a parent, as I had resolved that this problem was my responsibility. It was my job to figure out a way to save my son.

With every setback I felt increasingly despondent, more broken as a dad and as a man.

It was a vicious cycle. With every setback, I would intensify my efforts. With every failure, I would fall deeper into my own personal despair, while boosting my commitment. I was fighting a battle I couldn't win, systematically destroying myself in this effort.

On those occasions when my son would return to living on the streets, I would sometimes wake up in the middle of the night, my dreams interrupted by the nightmare I was living. Our family was under tremendous pressure and the situation was beginning to seem hopeless.

Sleep was the only escape and even then, I couldn't completely escape this.

Most interrupted nights I would go sit on the porch and pray in despair. I would pray for my son to come home and be safe. I would pray he would come back to us as he was as his younger self, cleaned up and drug-free, happy and full of promise. Often, I would add a second prayer in which I asked for help to deliver me through this crisis.

I consider myself a high-energy kind of guy, a can-do personality, someone who can usually figure things out. In this situation, there were no clear-cut answers, no obvious strategies or accomplishments for marking progress.

I was failing, I was falling apart, both physically and emotionally.

The situation escalated to the point where I started wishing for a heart attack to escape this misery flooding my life. I repeatedly told myself that I couldn't face another day dealing with all I was dealing with. Beaten down by the ongoing battle, I was beginning to give up on myself. I was losing hope, nearly to the point of giving up on my son, as well.

I was heart-broken.

Mile 3

I had hoped and prayed my son would embrace recovery.

Instead I heard him say time and time again: "I don't know if I even can do that. I don't want to detox. I don't want to go through withdrawal. I don't know if I can do this. Besides, what difference would it make?"

This created an intense inner conflict. I was doing everything I could to encourage my son to embrace the possibilities for his recovery, in finding hope for his life, while simultaneously battling my own sense of hopelessness and despair. I was determined there had to be a way for him out of this hell, even though I was starting to believe there wasn't any way out, other than to escape it.

My son's hopelessness, a hopelessness which was eroding his self-confidence, and self-love, had become my own. The hopelessness he was experiencing was the same hopelessness I was experiencing in relation to his troubles. Like my son, I was losing my way into a descent which was destroying my world order, including all faith, hope and trust.

I couldn't understand why he could not see beyond his despair and move toward recovery, even though, in my own despair, I struggled to see any promise for my own life. I had lost perspective and any sense of objectivity.

Typically, I would have never accepted this mindset from myself or someone else close to me. I expected more from him, and I expected more from myself. I would normally have demanded a better effort from me. I expected a fight and he knew it. I expected him to embrace recovery as the answer to the problems in his life, yet he was unable to stick with any of his efforts or make recovery work.

Sadly, the example I was currently living was in stark contradiction with the expectations I held for him and what I held for myself. Everything had become incomprehensible.

Our relationship was broken.

We butted heads many times over many things, not just over his recovery. We tangled over all the related drama and chaos which had penetrated our lives until it reached the point where we just stopped talking about the situation or his issues altogether. He stopped sharing where he was and there seemed to be nothing left to say.

When he attempted to quit using, he would try different programs, though always under his terms, to sustain his recovery. When those efforts fell apart, the cycle would begin all over again. When whatever he tried failed I'd be upset with myself, and in turn I'd be upset with him. He would get frustrated with himself, then he would get frustrated with me.

It was a vicious, toxic cycle perpetuated over months that turned into years.

What I didn't realize then, but discovered much later, was my son's addiction was a symptom of a much larger issue, the pain of his own personal trauma. His personal trauma was grounded in his fundamental belief he was not good enough and he would never be good enough. His internal story caused him to seek out ways to feel better, to numb the pain associated with his own personal inadequacies.

Alcohol or drugs are often used to numb pain or escape trauma. What may have started as an experiment, or a way of fitting in with peers by using drugs, can become a way to escape uncomfortable emotions. Using a substance to change a way of feeling is one of the drivers of addiction.

As a person moves toward feeling feel less pain they begin to lose touch with other emotions, as well. The loss of self-respect or, of self-love often being the high price they pay. Fear, pain, loss and uncomfortable feelings are joined by self-loathing, and a rejection of those around them.

Mile 4

Trauma is not the only underlying issue behind addiction tendencies.

Another contributor to substance use disorder is co-existing mental disorders. Individuals who have experiences with mental health or behavioral issues as a child, sadly have a higher propensity for substance use.

Substance use disorder can be instigated from an injury or condition for which prescription pain-killers or opioids have been provided. The prescribing of opioids for pain relating to wisdom tooth extractions or sports injuries can lead to an addiction to the medication.

The medical and the parental community is still catching up on the issue with prescribing opioids to treat pain in young adults. Thankfully, the medical community has started to decrease initial prescription amounts or eliminated the prescribing of them completely. This issue is now being more widely discussed and more remedies are being pursued which we hope will decrease the number of children and young adults impacted by these highly addictive substances.

Substance use disorder occurs when the pleasure receptors rewire the brain. Once these pleasure receptors discover the ideal positive, rewarding experience from a drug or activity, it desires that resource to the point it becomes the only thing the brain craves. Once this experience is locked into the brain's memory, it becomes very difficult to let it go.

This exhilaration effect explains the drivers behind all forms of addiction, especially sex, video gaming, gambling, and substance use, where the pleasure receptor in the brain responds to the positive experience and demands more of it.

I spent years putting parental pressure on my son for him to get clean and straighten out his life without really understanding what was really going on inside his mind and his body.

I had no clue as to what was behind his substance abuse and I had even less insight as to what was getting in the way of his recovery. All I knew and believed was something had to change and I couldn't understand what was keeping him stuck in the place he was in.

I did not comprehend the journey of recovery, the full complexity of the addicted brain, and the mechanisms which drive people to keep using, long after they consciously wish they could stop.

I struggled with the perception of addiction many people have, that one chooses to continue their addiction even though they say they want to stop.

I did not understand the workings of brain chemistry behind addiction, which hardwires an addiction into their system.

As a result, my frustration grew with my son's seeming willingness to maintain a habit which was slowly, systematically destroying him, and me. It was from a position of utter frustration, of overwhelming anguish, of complete brokenness, I decided the only way anything was going to change, was to change myself. It was a decision that would prove incredibly and powerfully transformational.

Mile 5

What are you going to do about it?

One night as I was sitting on the porch, repeating my middle of the night, interrupted sleep and prayer routine, I said to myself; "How many times are you going to do this before you do something different?" It was a call to action, a call to change. And change I did. Once I declared, "I've got to stop doing this! I've got to stop being in his journey," it took very little time before I took action. I made a commitment to ride my bike for an hour a day for one-hundred consecutive days. The purpose of the rides was to challenge myself to do something I was not certain I could complete.

You do not know what you are capable of until you challenge yourself to do something you have never done before.

I intentionally created this challenge to mirror, in a small way, the pressure put on my son to embrace recovery in his life. I knew he did not feel or think he could make recovery work, but I saw him making attempts and it inspired me to tackle my own challenge. I needed to do something to restore my sense of confidence in my own pursuits, to break out of my own broken hole. I needed to prove my own self-efficacy and I needed an accomplishment.

Confidence is the belief that you can and will find the way to do something, it is not limited to the belief you are already good at something.

Commitment is tenacity, it is relentless, and it is powerful. Confident commitment provides courage in the unknown. Courage is the force in a moment of great stress to engage in a healthy response and a constructive course of action in conflict.

Courage is something we all have within us, even if we don't know it, trust it, or rely on it. Courage is often the resource we trust in to help us follow the best route through, or away from a real or imagined threat. Without courage, we would remain stuck, unable to move forward.

When it came to my one-hundred-day challenge, it was in the confidence of my commitment I was able to courageously embrace the challenge and move forward into the unknown.

The point of the rides was to embrace the challenge and experience the journey under the pressure I placed on myself, for myself.

I did not know when I started my first rides if, or how, I could do the one-hundred-day challenge and complete those many, many rides. But this was about embracing something I knew was needed to help me rise above the enormous burden I had been under for years. These daily cycling events were powerfully meditative. It wasn't about the exercise or heartbeats per minute but rather it was about commitment and shifting my attention away from the crisis- oriented lifestyle I had been living.

From the first bike ride, I had taken the first step toward finding hope and opportunity. Interestingly, the quote which was captured on the very first bike ride in the one-hundred-day challenge demonstrated my commitment to reclaim the life I desired to live. "No matter how dark the present appears, I choose to live for the promise of the future and to celebrate the opportunities created through my passion and my gifts." Thank goodness for this ride. It facilitated a transformation from where I was, in complete hopelessness, to where I desired to be, one of hope and opportunity.

100 days and 2,360 miles later...I accomplished my 100-day cycling challenge!

My son rode with me the last four miles of that ride. He was still in "active use" but he joined me on the ride because he thought it was a cool thing his dad was doing, and he wanted to support me. With the bike ride challenge completed, everything changed.

Everything changed not with my son's addiction, but with me and my life. My relationships, my energy, and my health all experienced significant shifts, despite the presence of my son's active addiction. I had effectively removed myself from the ongoing chaos of my son's addiction and had shifted my focus on living the best life I could.

Mile 6

It wasn't change, in the sense that everything suddenly became better.

It was change, in the sense that everything became less overwhelming. Situations became more manageable. I was not only responding more appropriately but recovering much more quickly when things did go off the rails. Situations at home, at work and with my son slowly but surely started to slow down.

Before the bike rides, I reacted to every little event as though it were connected to the elephant of addiction in the life of our family. I noticed after each bike ride, I was acting more appropriately and responding versus reacting to situations. My responses were becoming more measured and my communication was becoming increasingly calm. I was making progress and was becoming increasingly aware of the positive changes. In the face of stress or conflict, I would step back, take a moment to pause, reflect, assess the situation, and provide a more appropriate and thoughtful response to the situation. The more I became engaged in this approach, the better my responses, and the more confident I became in managing life's adversities. I then had a breakthrough that altered the course of our relationship.

I remember telling my son, after the cycling challenge was completed, I wasn't going to be actively involved in managing his recovery. His response was, "good, now I will have to focus on it."

Even though he wasn't in recovery at the time, the message was clear – I had taken on the responsibility for his recovery. Why would he work on something if he didn't have to? I was doing the work for him and wondering why he wasn't getting the results.

When my son told me he had backed off his own recovery because of my heavy involvement I was shocked. Only then did I fully realize how much of his recovery I had been managing. I would drive him where ever he needed to go, to make certain he got to work, stayed in compliance with his legal obligations, and I took him to his recovery meetings and appointments.

Recovery is work. It requires commitment and the consistency of daily application.

As with any major life change, it is never easy and can only be accomplished when the person seeking change makes and lives out their commitment to get where they desire to go.

Few people change adverse life behaviors unless they experience the impact of their choices in their life.

Protecting my son and doing the work for him was protecting him from any responsibility for his substance use disorder and path forward. I had to let go and I did.

Mile 7

Every bike ride provided me with an insightful revelation for me to internalize.

After every ride, I would sit down and journal my reflections and make note of any new insights. Meditation often brings clarity. It allows the mind to relax, the cluttered mind to clear, creating a space for fresh, new ideas to emerge.

These cycling related reflections helped change everything.

When I started my rides, my life was in complete physical and emotional chaos. If you think of my life as an office, it was a complete mess with papers, books, and notes strewn everywhere. It would be impossible to find anything or get any work done in the office of my life. When I got off the bike, my office was in complete order. I didn't have all the answers, but I appreciated what I had learned and experienced up to this point and how to best utilize it.

I often encourage others to consider taking on a life changing challenge, though I don't require them to do what I did. While a big challenge was incredibly impactful for turning my life around, it may not work for everyone. However, changing your experience with your loved one's addiction will require some form of commitment on your part. If they won't change their problematic behaviors, the only way your life will change is if you adjust or alter yours.

I encourage you to take a moment to examine your life and define where you are and where you desire to be. First, envision where you want to be, daydream, scrapbook, draw, write poetry or go for a lengthy walk or jump on a bike. Free up your mind.

As you examine these two situations, your present and your future, you can identify the gap and explore what you, yourself, need to do to get there.

This is how the one-hundred-day challenge came to fruition as I sat on the porch and assessed my life.

It facilitated a change which, to this day, continues to provide me with incredible lessons. It sounds like work and it is. Then, so is recovery. If we expect our children to do the work to change their life in relation to their addiction, the best example we can set for them is to do our own work.

Mile 8

I discovered a new path and everything began to change.

I remember it as though it were yesterday, the shock I felt knowing one of my children was battling a heroin addiction. I also remember the painful, confusing journey that followed. With the benefit of hindsight and eight years on this journey, I have learned a great deal — about recovery, addiction, self-care and being my adult child's dad. As I shared earlier, once I started on a new and different path, everything began to change.

Once everything started to slow down, I began to trust my own learning and growth process.

Getting to this place wasn't an overnight event, it was a series of continuous personal educational experiences and activities which brought me here. As part of my commitment to share the life changing experiences of my one-hundred-day challenge, I created a non-profit organization called 100Pedals. The mission for the organization was to provide parents and other family members with the tools and resources to navigate the chaos of a loved one's addiction.

It was, and is, my plan to guide parents through their addiction struggles without having to experience some of the heartbreak and failure that I did.

One of my first initiatives was to go on the road with my bike and meet with parents at events, parent group meetings, churches, schools, and treatment facilities. I would throw my bike on the back of my car and drive around a region of the country for several weeks, riding in the morning with a local cycling group and speaking in the afternoon or evening to parents. This program has become an annual event.

In 2016, I changed the program. Instead of driving to cities and cycling locally, I decided to ride my bike across the country. The first cycling trip was a ride from Santa Monica, CA to Chicago, IL and then back to my old hometown of Detroit, MI. This ride took me the length of legendary Route 66. I would bike over sixty miles a day, six days a week. This 2500-mile ride was an incredible outreach project, as I connected with individuals looking to share their addiction experiences and stories.

While the level of event related interactions was relatively predictable, I could not have anticipated the incredible interactions which occurred as I was riding my bike during the day. People would pull up to me, flag me down, or greet me in a hotel or restaurant parking lot to engage and talk about addiction. It was incredible.

Mile 9

Eventually, you find yourself somewhere else.

When I was cycling Route 66, from Santa Monica, CA to Chicago, IL, I came upon a fellow cyclist just outside of Amarillo, TX.

He was on the same route, except he was heading in the other direction. As we shared stories of our motivations and experiences cycling this legendary road, he shared something incredibly profound, "I ride every day. I ride as little as forty miles and as much as one hundred. Every day I get up and ride. After a couple of days of riding, I find myself somewhere else."

His words were probably the most inspirational, memorable of the entire seventy-day Route 66 adventure.

When we are in a dark period in our life, we seek the most immediate path out. Once we decide things aren't working as we expect, we often reactively change course, define a new path and go through the entire process all over again.

I loved how my fellow adventurous cyclist simplified change. It is most reflective of the original one-hundred-day challenge. I didn't know where I was going, what it was going to accomplish, or how it was going to change my life, if at all.

All I knew is I needed to do something. I made a commitment to change and trusted the path.

After one hundred days, I was somewhere else, and it has led to so much more.

If you are reading this book, you are on a growth journey. You cannot get there overnight. Change is the byproduct of a continuous series of committed steps. Moving forward requires sustained commitment, a grittiness, and it requires trust and faith in yourself. After a while, you may not be where you want to be; but, with consistent effort, you will. Embrace the power which comes from having confidence in this truth!

Mile 10

The following recommendations are based on reflection of my journey.

I am sharing steps which may or may not, necessarily, work for you; but, I believe if you internalize them and think about them carefully, they are likely activities which, deep down inside, you already know you need to do.

All you simply need is to decide you are at the point where you say: "Yes, I've got to find a better way to parent a child with an addiction, not only for myself, but for them."

Engage and commit to a steep learning curve

Before doing anything, the best activity a parent can engage in is to gather information to more precisely understand what you are dealing with and discover all options available to you. Addiction is a complex and complicated problem. Despite your fears, concerns, and emotions of guilt and shame, asking for help and educating yourself before rushing into action is crucial.

When I went into rescue mode, it was reactive. It was unhealthy, it was self-protecting. I had no idea what I was dealing with.

I didn't know who to call or who I could trust. I determined I could and needed to figure out how to fix this on my own. I was sadly mistaken.

What I know now is the most important step is to go into learning mode. If your child received a prognosis they had a serious illness like cancer, you would research the issue, ask as many questions as possible, maybe even seek out a second or third opinion. You would ask friends who you know or trust that had similar experiences, reaching out to them for perspective, information or recommendations.

Addiction is no different, except we are afraid to publicly share our struggle. As a result, we end up, like I did, taking this on ourselves. Engaging in learning, in gathering information, and utilizing the resources which are available to you are essential, crucial activities. You need not do this alone and you are not helping yourself or others if you try to. A good place to start is with the Partnership for Drug Free Kids (www.drugfree.org). The Partnership offers a wide range of informational programs for parents of children of all ages, and resource material for prevention education, as well as for dealing with substance abuse issues in the family.

Mile 11

Do not expect or seek out a quick solution or an easy result.

As you do your research, especially in talking with other parents who are on similar paths, you will soon learn that treatment and recovery is a process.

The process is more complex than simply arranging a 30-day stint at a rehab facility or encouraging your child to become part of a 12-step program.

What you are dealing with is much more complex than simply committing to recovery and going to treatment, where everything magically happens. The process is hard work, with ups and downs, successes and setbacks, relapses, punch-in-the-gut disappointments, and incredibly exciting breakthroughs.

Prepare yourself for a roller coaster, emotional journey and do your homework, first. You will be much better off focusing on the long-term recovery journey than placing your hopes on a one-size-fits-all or quick fix recovery program.

A quick result that returns your child's life and your family to the old normal is an unrealistic expectation. I encourage you to be prepared to shift into a new normal and begin to adjust to the reality that most everything in your life will experience some form of change.

Be wary of people promoting or assuring you thirty-day treatment programs are sufficient.

A thirty-day program is a good start, helps guide your loved one effectively through the early post-detox recovery; but, it is minimally effective in sustaining ongoing long-term recovery. There is much more planning, work, and structure required to sustain a long-term recovery beyond a month-long treatment program.

This is where the education process pays dividends. It saves you much confusion and frustration. Learn to understand what is involved in an effective, comprehensive treatment and recovery program, prepare for the long-term journey, and manage your actions and expectations accordingly.

Mile 12

Commit yourself and your family to the recovery process.

Addiction involves all members of the family. Even though you may have just one child dealing with substance use disorder, the entire family is affected.

Too many parents think all they need to do is send their child to a treatment program and everything will be okay. If it were only that simple.

Substance use disorder is a family disease and the family needs to be involved with their own treatment recovery program as well. This is often a challenging concept for parents and family members. The conflict comes as parents and loved ones often say, "I am not the one with the problem." This is true but it is also a limiting perspective.

While not always a popular opinion, I firmly believe the family needs to be completely engaged in the recovery and education process, including their own "recovery program," to help them be more aware of what their loved one is experiencing and working on. Substance use and successful recovery are heavily influenced by our environment. This is not to say the family is responsible for their loved one's addiction, or for triggering their relapses. However, as families are closely engaged with each other, often sharing or creating a common environment, family members need to understand how they may influence and trigger behaviors and emotions.

Engaging in a family education and recovery process also helps everyone better understand the issue, brings enlightenment to each person's own behaviors, and better prepares each family member to be a constructive partner in the recovery process.

While the person battling their addiction is responsible for their recovery, the process is enhanced immeasurably when the family is better equipped to support and encourage them.

Mile 13

While your life will be dramatically altered through this experience, your child's drug addiction doesn't have to completely disrupt your life.

If it does, it means you have lost, or are in the process of losing, control of your life. If you learned anything from reading my journey up to this point, you'll realize this is neither healthy nor productive.

Despite the chaos around you give priority to taking care of yourself. Hopefully, you already have healthy routines in your life which sustain you. I not, begin to. These consistent routines could be morning walks, working out at the gym, date night with your spouse, quiet time, or group activities at church or in the neighborhood.

Whatever routines you have in place for your mental, physical, emotional or spiritual health need to be maintained and strengthened. These activities are what ground you and recharge you. Too many parents interrupt their healthy routines or completely alter their schedules and priorities in the face of a child's addiction.

Allowing substance use and addiction to move your life into a place of personal imbalance is unhealthy.

You need time for yourself to meditate, reflect, or recharge. Safe, reliable activities that bring you pleasure and stability need to be protected. Changing healthy routines to focus on your child's recovery is unhealthy and can eventually be toxic for both you and your child.

Self-care may seem to be a luxurious gift you are giving to yourself; but, it impacts how you engage with others and how you respond to the challenges of addiction in your life. You are doing it for you, but everyone benefits when you do and suffers when you don't.

Mile 14

The trap most parents fall into is their belief that they need to help manage their child's recovery. This is a mistake.

When a parent begins to assume responsibility for managing their child's recovery it sends two messages to the child: *they aren't capable of managing their own recovery; and, they don't have to be responsible for their recovery.*

Parents need to recognize who is responsible for their child's recovery and empower their child to own it. Otherwise, their child will struggle to embrace their role and accountability for the outcomes associated with it.

This is a very difficult shift for parents, especially those who have a tendency to be hands-on and controlling. But, it is critically important to recognize, not only why this is important, but what is behind the parental behavior.

It requires accountability and individual responsibility, and experiences with accomplishment and setbacks. There are consequences for not being responsible or accountable in life, not just in recovery. For recovery to work, to be sustainable, the person in recovery needs to own their work. It cannot be accomplished or achieved effectively when someone else is doing some, or all of it. When mom or dad are involved in their child's recovery, they are doing the work, they are taking responsibility. When this happens, the boundaries get blurred, often crossed, and the child usually ends up failing in their recovery because they haven't learned how to own it; or, didn't have to own it.

Fear drives parents into crossing the line into managing their child's recovery.

Anything which seems to be a setback, or a potential, horrible consequence resulting from their child's inaction draws parents into helping sustain the recovery process. They fear the outcome, the failure in recovery, or having to start over and get drawn into rescuing the recovery from relapse.

If your child is not doing the work, they are not in recovery, and all you are doing is delaying the inevitable and denying the obvious.

Release your fears, release control, and let them manage their recovery, including the experiences associated with not being responsible for their recovery related activities. I know how difficult it is to not get emotionally wrapped up into the addiction situation from the onset. You may feel like you need to do something now. You are correct, but it is not what you think or have likely done in the past.

Instead, taking a reasoned approach in response to the situation is critically important. A deliberate and thoughtful approach now will significantly benefit you and your child in the long-run.

Remember, recovery from addiction is a long-term process.

Mile 15

Respond to the situation, rather than emotionally react to it.

Every family goes through significant turbulence and chaos in dealing with the choices and actions of an addicted child.

Whether it is violent confrontations, deceptions or criminal activity it doesn't matter, addiction introduces highly charged, emotional situations to everyone involved.

The family dynamic is turned into an emotional quagmire when faced with the addiction-related choices of the child. The way to deal most successfully with these situations is not to react in the moment, responding to them with clarity of purpose and intention.

You will be placed in difficult situations, complicated by intense emotional energy. There will be times when everything seems to be spiraling out of control, nothing makes sense, and everyone is angry, hurt, and confused. Personal reflection, self-care, education, and your personal recovery process all come together to make a difference in these circumstances.

It involves committing to discovering different ways to respond, forgiving yourself when it doesn't go as planned and reflecting on how you will do things differently next time. You will succeed over time in bringing healthy energy into chaotic situations.

It is incredibly hard to watch a child, your child, go through their personal struggles, as a result from their use of drugs.

It is terribly difficult to witness them experiencing and participating in behaviors which are chaotic, destructive and have the potential for deadly consequences. It is sometimes too easy to get pulled into the drama of their journey and lose your way in the process.

I don't live in complete and total peace every day; but, I often discover ways to find peace in my life, despite the chaos, on a regular basis.

Mile 16

Practice selfless listening.

Shifting from telling to listening was one of the most impactful behaviors I engaged in with my son. Listening created a safe space for my son to begin to share what he was going through on his journey.

His honest sharing provided me a perspective I had previously struggled to accept or understand, mainly because I was so busy telling him what I wanted him to do and what I expected him to do.

I had become good at sharing my perspectives, expectations and viewpoint. Unfortunately, I was missing critical information, which was all my son was experiencing. I had determined he had no sense of how messed up his life was or what he needed to do to turn it around, so I chose to repeatedly remind him, without ever giving him a safe place to be upfront with me.

Most of the parents I engage with share all different ways they tell, encourage, and remind their children about what they need to do, how they need to change their life, or where they are failing in their recovery efforts. Sadly, all this confrontational telling only brings the parents' perspectives into the conversation.

While we feel the need to re-emphasize the critical importance of engaging in the necessary activities for our children to get their life back on track, all this telling reminds them of the many ways they are continually failing in their life and falling short of our expectations for them.

For many people struggling with substance use disorder, confrontational telling only reinforces the hopelessness they are experiencing in their lives rather than serving to inspire or encourage them to interrupt the path their life is on.

Selfless listening involves making a commitment to create a safe place for your child or loved one to share the struggles of their addiction journey.

By creating this judgement-free zone, they are encouraged to openly share where they are, what they are experiencing, what their challenges and frustrations are, and what they perceive to be obstacles to their recovery path.

The key component of this activity or behavior is your commitment to listen without interruption, without criticism or condemnation, without trying to solve, coach or inspire. This provides your child or loved one with a space to openly and freely share what they are experiencing.

Mile 17

Selfless listening accomplishes several powerful outcomes.

1. **Perspective**:

   It provides you with fresh insights into the other's journey; information which was previously unknown to you. While you had made assumptions about what you believed you knew, this perspective was based on your filter, your perceptions, and your opinions.

   When your loved one shares exactly what they see, think, feel and experience from their world, you are offered the gift of new, previously unknown insights. Discovering their truth is a powerful and eye-opening experience for you as their parent.

2. **Connection:**

   The minute I made a commitment to listen and worked at this behavior, my son noted the change in me. After a while, he began to trust my commitment and more freely shared with me. This authentic sharing, which goes both ways, brought us closer together.

Many parents mourn the loss of the relationship as they find themselves disconnected or distanced by substance abuse from their children. Much of this disconnect is the outcome of our one-dimensional interactions as we engage in our recovery-centric parental mission.

As I shifted from a recovery-centric behavior to the love and acceptance model associated with listening, my son and I began to reconnect.

3. **Healing**:

Once we have created a safe zone which facilitates authentic connection, selfless listening begins the process of healing. All the words, all the fears, all the expressed frustrations and criticisms begin to be put behind us. The more I listened, the more I learned, and the more I learned, the higher level my awareness was.

This awareness was not only limited to what I didn't know or understand about my son's journey, but also revealed a great deal about me as his dad.

Some of these discoveries were painful and shocking. The lessons these insights provided offered me an opportunity to discover who I was as a dad and how I could alter my behaviors to be the dad my son needed me to be.

This was a significant life and healing lesson, one which could have not been facilitated if I had not been listening.

Mile 18

Substance use disorder defined.

Addiction is a primary, chronic disease of brain reward, motivation, memory and related circuitry. Dysfunction in these circuits leads to characteristic biological, psychological, social and spiritual manifestations. This is reflected in an individual pathologically pursuing reward and/or relief by substance use and other behaviors.

Addiction is characterized by inability to consistently abstain, impairment in behavioral control, and craving, diminished recognition of significant problems with one's behaviors and interpersonal relationships, and a dysfunctional emotional response.

Like other chronic diseases, addiction often involves cycles of relapse and remission. Without treatment or engagement in recovery activities, addiction is progressive and can result in disability or premature death. ~ American Society of Addiction Medicine

With the benefit of scientific study, we are ever expanding our knowledge of the complexities of substance use disorder, as a chronic mental health condition that affects brain and body functions.

Ongoing research continues to provide greater insights regarding the wide range of effective treatment modalities that are available to those seeking treatment and recovery.

Substance use disorder affects all demographics from adolescents to senior citizens, from low income families to the upper middle-class communities. However, the young are particularly susceptible to the addiction/substance use disorder as their brains are not fully developed and it is for this reason that they are the most vulnerable to harmful substances, some of which pose irreparable damage to cognitive function, and even the ability to feel fully or realize their potential.

Mile 19

Substance use disorder is a mental health disorder.

It occurs when the pleasure receptors in the brain develop an unhealthy attachment to a particular activity or substance. This attachment can become an obsession for the pleasure receptors in the brain with a single experience.

Once the brain has defined this experience as most desirable, or essential, the brain obsessively focuses on repeating this experience, often referred to as "chasing the high." This obsession becomes an all-encompassing demand driven by the brain.

Despite all the adverse experiences or outcomes associated with continued use, the brain continues to seek the pleasure associated with the substance or activity, ignoring all other consequences or results.

When talking about substance use disorder, the simplest way to explain it, is the brain gets hijacked. What gets hijacked is the logical side of the brain, where lessons and experience temper choices and decisions. Someone with substance use disorder has the logical component of their mind overridden by the pleasure side.

This helps explain why addiction driven behaviors are so hard to understand. Some of the behaviors someone with substance use disorder displays defies logic.

One specific part of the brain has hijacked the whole mind in pursuit of the one thing which provides its ultimate pleasure or relief.

Take note that substance use disorder is not limited to substances, it can also manifest itself in other behaviors. Gambling and sex addiction, for example, are behaviors not associated with any specific substances, yet they have the same detrimental impact on a life as drug and alcohol addiction do. This is because these activities provide pleasure to the brain which can trigger an unhealthy attachment to them.

Mile 20

To help expand your understanding of substance use disorder, let's take a close look at two most common misperceptions.

Myth #1: It is a choice.

Yes, a person can choose to engage in an activity, illegal or not, illicit or not.

They made a choice to engage in that activity, they should have known the risk. All true, technically correct, but an oversimplification of the real problem.

No one chooses their addiction. Their addiction chooses them.

Disorder means something is not in order. Say you are going over the speed limit while driving down the road and the tire blows out. The sudden flat, combined with excessive speed results in your inability to manage your vehicle and you crash into another vehicle.

In the "it's a choice" view, an argument could be made that you made the choice to drive recklessly when you sped down the road and are responsible for carelessness and causing an accident.

Under the unintended consequences perspective, you had no idea your tires were at risk of blowing out. If you had, you would have been more careful. Was the accident the result of recklessness or an unfortunate accident? You decide.

We have no idea what triggers are lurking in our brain. It is only when we are exposed to something which triggers us, do we discover what has been hidden in there. Our tires seem normally worn and manageable until something causes them to blow out. This doesn't justify the initial choice, nothing can. However, we have all made bad decisions.

I have been alcohol free since 2001. I never thought of my drinking as a problem or an issue. I knew I loved to drink. I knew I drank more than most people. And, I was aware I tested the limits of reasonable drinking.

I went to a therapist one day seeking help for my continued depression. I had a great career, was financially successful, a wife who loved me and three great kids. Yet, I was miserable inside. When she asked me about my drinking, I told how much I was consuming at home on a weekly basis. Her response was, "so you're self-medicating." I had to ask her what that meant. Essentially, I was using alcohol to help me feel better, to move beyond the garbage in my head. My drinking was helping me cope with psychological issues I was struggling to deal with and I was using alcohol to numb out or blur.

Fortunately, my drinking never caused me permanent difficulty in my life. When I honestly look back on my path, my drinking created a few detours, but I never saw my self-medicating as a problem. After all, I enjoyed drinking, it made me feel better. I continued to drink, oblivious to the potential problems it could create in my life. This didn't mean I got off without some damage. When I asked my children about my drinking, they all said the same thing. They don't remember any specific issues except were forthcoming in telling me that they liked sober dad better than drinking dad.

At one point in my life, I chose to drink. I liked it. It worked. It numbed my pain. And, even though it didn't lead to a massive, chaotic shift in my life, I can look back through my sober lens today and identify areas where I came dangerously close to blowing it all up. I had no idea and I had no control. The visit to the therapist saved my life. On that visit I discovered my real issues were related to my drinking. It came at a fortuitous time where I was incredibly motivated to change my life. I got lucky. I found recovery before it became a more serious issue. I learned my tires were worn before I even got on the road.

Mile 21

Myth #2: People can stop using if they really want to.

Sadly, it is not as simple as that. A great deal goes into recovery from substance use disorder. Deciding to stop is only the first step in a very difficult and challenging process. According to The National Institute on Drug Abuse: "Long-term drug use results in significant changes in brain function that can persist long after the individual stops using drugs." This explains why many people say; "Relapse is part of the recovery process." It isn't just about deciding to stop and going into extended, long-term recovery. The process is much more complex and complicated than that and willpower is a very small piece of the solution.

It is critically important, to revisit and understand the brain's control of the situation. Recovery is more than a choice, it is a complicated process of detox, short term recovery, extended healing, and long-term care. Stopping only means the battle to remap or rewire the brain, and the difficult work, has just begun.

In the past, I was reluctant to share my own recovery journey from alcohol, because I felt like it was too easy, and, in my mind, I didn't do any of the hard work I watched my son and others go through in finding their long-term recovery.

My therapist challenged me to give up drinking before we could even begin therapy. Her message was clear, "I will treat you, but I will not work with you if you continued to self-medicate." I had a choice, quit drinking and get help, or live the life I was living.

I made a decision, I was going to stop drinking. I stopped and never went back. At least that is how I initially remembered it. Unfortunately, this simplified version memory about my own recovery created a false perception about the recovery process, one which others embrace about how recovery works. Upon closer inspection, my recovery wasn't as simple or easy as I historically had defined it.

From my recovery experience, I looked at my son with the same confusion and frustration others experience as we attempt to understand why recovery is so difficult to sustain. After all, if I made a choice and simply stopped drinking, why can't you stop using? I carried my critical attitude around for some time because I didn't really understand the bigger picture, even when it came to understanding my own recovery.

I didn't just stop drinking, I did the hard work required to sustain long-term recovery. It took a lot of personal reflection to realize I did a lot more work than I originally gave myself credit for. I saw a therapist once a week for two months, then took a sabbatical from work and went on a thirty-day retreat to focus specifically on the issues behind my addiction. During that thirty-day retreat, I lived by myself, only interacting with my therapist daily, and completed some intense therapy related assignments. When I returned, I saw my therapist once a week for another eighteen months. In hindsight, I didn't stop drinking simply because I decided to, I was able to stop drinking because I was afforded the appropriate support and guidance once I made an all-in commitment to my recovery.

My all-in commitment was the key. There is a powerful, yet unknown differentiation between going through the motions of a recovery program and committing to do recovery. This differing factor exists in our internal mindset, a definitive mind shift reflecting an all-in, do-what-it-takes commitment. This intangible differentiator cannot be explained or quantified. Finally, making a commitment is the perfect place to begin, however, having access to the resources necessary to support and sustain recovery, as I did when I quit drinking, is an essential component of the whole process.

I hear the same story, similar experiences from others who have found long-term recovery: "There was something about the time I found long-term recovery which was different. I can't explain it, but I knew this was it for me."

Mile 22

The whole concept of recovery can be frustrating for loved ones and over-simplified by outsiders.

Time and again, I have witnessed my son and others approach recovery with limited success. There were many times I watched him go into treatment, convinced he was ready, only to experience this feeling of failure with another relapse. As much as he or I believed he was ready, he wasn't.

I wish I knew the secret formula which guaranteed going to recovery would become a commitment to long-term recovery. I don't. All I know is that there is more to extended recovery than simply choosing it.

There are no simple answers to complicated problems and substance use disorder is one of those complex issues not readily solved by simple answers. Here are some references where you can look further into physiological and mental health, including the health of the brain in relation to the intake of various drugs.

https://www.drugabuse.gov/related-topics/addiction-science
https://www.centeronaddiction.org/addiction
https://www.projectknow.com/research/addiction-warning-signs/

Mile 23

We live in a society unaware the extent of our individual addictions.

We have become accustomed to quick fix, feel good, instant gratification resources. We expect, even demand, simple and sometimes, pain free options for solving our daily problems or making our life easier to cope or manage.

There is a pill for everything. We look to our doctors to give us a prescription to help us sleep, to keep us awake, to calm our nerves, to lose weight, to manage our pain, and even to have sex.

According to the *Journal of Pain;* "Americans consume prescription opioids at a greater rate than any other population in the world" and not because we are in more physical pain than other countries.

We come home from work and self-medicate with a "double on the rocks" or glasses of wine or get high on pot.

Unfortunately, too many of these addictive activities have become normalized and accepted. Not all of them are addictions for us, but many of them reflect addictive tendencies if we carefully examined and understood their impact and necessity. Even so, they are defended and protected because they are legal, even if their usage reflects addictive dependence.

Whenever I point out these perspectives, there is always someone willing to debate the reasonableness or rationale behind their behaviors and activities, angry at me for even being so bold as to label it an addiction.

It is only when an addiction to a drug of choice or behavior prevents us from functioning in society does one become judged, classified and stigmatized as an "addict."

An addiction to an illegal substance brings out a whole new level of stigma.

Over the past ten years, I have learned more than I desired or planned about the broad world of addiction — substance abuse, counseling, recovery, treatment, including the judicial and criminal justice systems' role in it. It is not the kind of subject matter I envisioned becoming overly knowledgeable about. I would never have volunteered to have this educational experience. Regardless, I am here just the same.

Before I began my addiction education, I was like most people when it came to this subject. I had no idea what substance use disorder was. I had my opinions. I had an image of what a person who had an addiction looked and acted like. I had my preconceptions as to what kind or type of person was "an addict." What I believed I knew and what I discovered were two entirely different realities.

Over the past ten years, I have made an important shift in developing an ability to express more empathy. Sadly, there are those who are simply allowing their predisposed opinions or perspectives to obstruct their ability to see this societal issue in for what it is. One of my primary objectives for this book and my ongoing outreach activities is to help educate those who struggle to understand or are unwilling to look at the issue of substance use disorder differently. A critical component of this educational effort is helping others better understand substance use disorder while recognizing how we can inhibit its growth in our society beyond governmental policy.

Education and prevention is a grass roots effort and will only be effective when most of our citizens understand what we are dealing with.

We know so much more about brain science, trauma, and addiction today than we did ten or twenty years ago. This provides us with tremendous opportunity to shift how we treat this illness and how we engage in prevention education activities. As pervasive as the issue is in our communities, there is still a great deal of work left, much of it grounded in a willingness to carefully examine our own thinking about addiction in our society, in our families and in our own behaviors. It is an uncomfortable examination but is one which will result in the greatest impact as awareness always facilitates the greatest change. Without a willingness to look at any issue from a fresh, open perspective, it is nearly impossible to illicit change.

From here, we will be looking at the issue of substance use disorder at different levels, shifting how we look at addiction and offering a place to have dialogue around improving societal responses to the issue in all aspects of our communities and families.

Mile 24

Young kids make bad decisions, they sometimes make stupid choices. Sadly, there can be some very unfortunate, sometimes permanent outcomes as a result.

With teenager years comes a youthful ignorance, which presents its own, interesting challenges, one of which is their belief they are invincible. Because the frontal cortex of the brain is not yet fully developed until they are in their twenties, teenagers are not in a place to fully grasp the level of risk they sometimes are taking. The ability to apply logic and reason to situations is also in this developmental phase.

This helps explain why the sad or unfortunate stories of other teens or young adults who have suffered dire consequences of their choices doesn't always resonate as possible outcomes in their own life. Try as we might, they don't believe any of the bad stuff we tell them could happen, could happen to them, because they cannot readily reason it could happen to them,

Young adults are willfully youthful, adventurous, or risk takers with a limited sense of the seriousness of their decisions or their consequences. Even if they do have some sense of negative outcome, they have no way of gauging or understanding what the worst result really means unless they experience the consequences of those choices. By then, it is too late to prevent it from happening and their life is forever changed.

There are other activities and emotions going on in the teenage mind. Becoming a young adult is a difficult emotional period in a person's life. In his book, *Beyond the Yellow Brick Road*, Bob Meehan describes the struggle of adolescence as a stage in life where "it is normal to feel bad."

According to Meehan, there are three basic stages of life: childhood, adolescence, and adulthood. Childhood is the period from birth to twelve years of age. Adulthood is the stage of life from eighteen to end of life. In the middle, from thirteen to eighteen, is adolescence.

Adolescence is this challenging period in our lives where we are in a physical and emotional transformation. Our bodies, our hormones, our brain are all going through massive development processes. Middle school and high school environments can be emotionally challenging as most everyone who is not an adult is struggling to feel comfortable with themselves, all the changes they are going through, and how they see themselves in these changes.

Most teenagers are eager to move out of adolescence. They look forward to the next stage of life, adulthood. Usually this is a transitive experience marked by graduation, getting out of the house, and going on to college. Imagine yourself as a teenager today, looking ahead to adulthood, finally free of all that represents adolescence. They begin to look to the future, ahead to becoming an adult and the possibilities associated with that. They examine the lives of the adults they are surrounded by at home, at school, at church, at their friends' houses and dream about what they will do, who they will become, where they will go.

What do they see? What do they experience? What gives them hope that life as an adult is any less challenging than being a teenager? What messages are we sharing with them, which offers hope and excitement for the life they are transitioning into?

To survive the struggles of adolescence, while searching for a reason to look forward to the future, many teenagers seek alternative ways to simply feel better. After all, this is what they really desire, to feel better. Some find this release and joy in sports, in their relationships, in academic accomplishment, in work, in other activities or in simply living. Others find it in bullying, sexual activity, or substance use. For some, it is a combination of both.

The rush which comes from these activities makes them feel better. Regardless of the behavior, for these teens the quest is the same. The source can be toxic or socially productive, it doesn't matter. The brain doesn't know the difference, it only knows what it wants, and this is to feel better, to numb or escape the pain.

Once the brain finds what it is looking for, it can hardwire that activity and desired result into the system. Whatever the activity is, it can become a driving obsession. This doesn't mean all teenagers are seeking ways to feel better or all teens will get trapped into a toxic behavior. The reality is, many teens are seeking ways to navigate the difficulties of adolescence which they experience at different, personal levels. Some of these choices can achieve immediate relief without any attachment and some become sustained addictions or obsessions.

Mile 25

Having a better understanding of the decisions and choices of our young adults and of their thoughts or emotions provides much needed perspective.

It also brings empathy into the discussion around their actions, rather than simply dismissing the behaviors as an example of poor choices.

When we engage with a young adult struggling with substance use disorder, we need to remember we are dealing with a young person who may have made a bad decision, but did not choose to be an addict.

Instead, we are dealing with a young adult whose brain has been hijacked and now are dealing with someone who is struggling with a mental health issue or brain disorder.

Now that we understand what we are dealing with, let's begin exploring responses to these critical questions:

How can we better educate our children on the dangers of substance abuse?

How can we improve our awareness and prevention activities in our communities and schools?

How can parents become more engaged in awareness and prevention education activities?

How can we better support parents with children who are struggling with substance use disorder?

Mile 26

Parents do the best they can with what they have.

Perfect parenting may be our objective, it is not reasonably attainable. As parents, we all make mistakes. Its part of the parenting process, doing the best you can with what you have. We all can reflect on a time when our parents made mistakes, some they even repeated over and over. All any parent has to offer their children is love and a commitment to do the best they can with what they have.

Have you ever struggled with the fear of making a bad parenting decision, or being concerned about how others saw you as a parent?

It is common for parents to fear being judged for their parenting decisions. It is from these fears and concerns some of our parenting decisions can be clouded. After all, the measuring stick for successful parenting is often measured by a single outcome, how our children turn out.

If our children stay out of trouble and become contributing citizens, the parent did their job and did it well. If the child is wildly successful, the parents must be proud, celebrating they have done a great job; and, if the child is a troublemaker, a criminal, a drug addict, well, something must have happened at home. Those poor parents. Wonder what happened there?

Let's get real, few parents really have complete control over their children and their choices. We would love to believe this and some try very hard to be in complete control. Bottom line is we can exert a lot of influence, but ultimately, we have very little control. Even in the best of parenting environments, children still have the ability, and sometimes do, make painful, destructive choices, few of which are a direct reflection on the parenting dynamic.

This does not mean parents are exempt from enhancing their skills as parents, especially in today's turbulent environment.

In my experience with family and substance use disorder, there are several areas where parents could be a better developmental resource to their children, where parents would benefit from awareness of their own behaviors on the developmental environment in their family, and how their active engagement in education and awareness programs does have influence and impact.

Here are a few key points:

- Parents need to be more proactively engaged in encouraging better choices.
- Parents need to be better educated on the risks associated with all substances, illicit or legal.
- Parents need to be better prepared, educated and warned of the dangers inherent in the drugs of choice of this generation.
- Parents need to be cognizant of their own patterns of addiction or dependency and recognize the need to change their life by taking on their own recovery program.
- Parents need to be actively involved in listening to their children and providing them a safe place to share their experiences and struggles.
- Parents need to be proactively receptive to accessing appropriate resources and proactively pursue information when they discover their child is struggling with substance use.

Mile 27

An actively, engaged parent will impact prevention and education efforts.

"In order to get ahead of this issue, we need the parents. We need the parents actively involved in awareness and prevention education programs." ~ Debbie Moak, Former Director, Arizona Governor's Office on Faith, Youth, and Family.

Having attended numerous parent education programs across the country, the level of participation is sadly and disappointing low. The responsibility for these education programs has been allocated to the schools and they are doing their very best with what they have. However, with parental participation levels at these education programs so low, there is little or no follow-up teaching on this subject at home. The other result is the parent has insufficient information to provide or conduct effective follow-up at home.

This represents a critical gap in our battle against substance use and substance use disorder. The next few segments in this mile seek to reemphasize the critical importance of education in both prevention and in crises. Parental education is critically important.

Discovering their child is struggling with an addiction triggers in parents a wild emotional combination made up of shock, guilt, fear or denial.

They often panic first, fearing their child may turn into one of those "addicts" so horrifically, incorrectly stereotyped on television. You know the ones. Shooting up in back alleys in the dark part of the city.

If people only knew how far off this stereotype really is. Most children are using drugs in the comfort of their middle or upper middle-class homes or in their neighborhood. If parents understood how far off their stereo-typed perceptions were, they might be more amenable to the real possibility that addiction could exist in their family and embrace an educational program to help minimize these prospects.

Or, they go into denial about what they are experiencing or being told about their child's situation. Using these same "addict" stereotypes as a benchmark, they cannot possibly see their child in this situation. After all, their child doesn't look like an addict, live like an addict, or dress like an addict. Their reactive defense mechanism allows them to see something other than the truth, because their visual image of an addict or someone with an addiction doesn't represent what they see or believe about their child's situation.

Or, they begin to engage in activities to protect the child, other members of the family, and the parents from condemnation and judgement. Their strategy for dealing with the situation is driven by their concerns that someone at school, church, work, or in the neighborhood may find out. Many parents go into damage control mode.

Nothing could be worse than people finding out that my kid is one of "those" children. They will judge me, abandon me, and ostracize me and my family. Nobody can find out.

Crippled by these reactive thoughts and fears, parents tend to make rushed, impulsive decisions. Their quest to quickly manage the problem before too much damage is done, or word gets out, often leads to reactive solutions rather than engaging in a consultative, collaborative learning and strategic process. When the primary objective is to keep the family "problem" out of the community gossip, making the treatment and recovery process more about protecting the family's good name, the child often doesn't receive the most appropriate treatment and recovery support at the most critical time.

Mile 28

Fear has a powerful ability to interrupt or prevent logical thought.

Fear is not a healthy place to operate from when identifying or defining substance use disorder treatment strategies. Fearing we may have failed as parents often leads to overreactions, blame, and cover-ups. It leads to bad decisions in the quest for the quick fix. Fear enables parents to make choices to protect and react, rather than appropriately respond to the issue.

Parents can make treatment and recovery decisions driven by fear and expediency. This doesn't always lead to finding the best program for their child. It is easy to be seduced by a program which they can afford, or which appear to offer all the best resources for their child. This doesn't always insure their child is going to the best program for them.

Without doing any research, it is hard to really know which program is best for your child. When searching for the treatment resources, it is critical for parents to do their homework. Not all treatment programs are the same, have the same reputations or results, and not all offer the same resources. Finding the treatment program which will work best for your child cannot be discovered when fear and expediency are two of the decision-making drivers.

There are organizations which pitch the value of their treatment programs in a manner which specifically plays upon desperate parents. They can tell a great story, but it doesn't mean this is the place for your child.

I have participated in the sharing of far too many parent stories celebrating their child finally going to recovery, only to find the program, the facility, or the culture wasn't what they had hoped or expected. Their next experience is often a story of leaving the facility, relapsing and beginning the recovery process all over again.

Identifying the best treatment facility for your child requires diligent research and education. Parents are encouraged to ask around, talk to other parents and families, and obtain recommendations. Move past your fears and your quest for expedient answers to search out the best resource for your child. Keep in mind, even though you may place your child in the ideal facility, it does not guarantee recovery. Your child must still be willing to do the work once they get there.

Mile 29

When I found out my son had a serious heroin addiction, I began to examine myself as a potential contributor to the problem.

Two emotions which have a powerful influence on a parent's interactions with their child are guilt and shame. Guilt is this sense of having done something wrong, that we are somehow responsible for this situation. Shame is the feeling there is something inherently wrong with me, in the sense that I should be able to fix it, or make it go away. In this section, I will focus on these two emotions and how they impact our behaviors with our addicted child.

When I first learned of my son's addiction and his related struggles, I had this sense of personal responsibility, or guilt, that perhaps I did something wrong or missed something which may have led to this issue. I attempted to compensate for my perceived past failings and make up for them by immersing myself into his addiction and recovery, almost to a fault.

My guilt-ridden behaviors didn't make the situation any better. I was desperate to fix it to relieve my guilt. But, my son didn't need me involved so I could make up for my perceived parenting deficiencies, he needed an emotionally healthy, balanced dad. He needed a dad who could support and encourage him, not save him or rescue him.

Once I got out of the way, my son took responsibility for his recovery. Many of his decisions and choices shifted. Once I stopped trying to manage his life out of my own sense of guilt he came to realize and experience the impact he could have on his life.

When it comes to shame, many parents struggle to understand why their love, their connection to their child and their commitment are not enough to change the situation. They are convinced they should be able to fix this. When they can't, when they don't, there must be something wrong with them.

Shaming ourselves is neither healthy nor productive. I get it. It is hard not to experience a sense of inadequacy when everything we try doesn't seem to work. For me, the more I worked at it, the worse it seemed to be. The worse it got, the harder I worked at it. It became an obsession. Every setback or failure added to my sense of inadequacy or my incapacity as a parent. The shame of failure weighed heavily on me.

What freed me from guilt and shame was finally understanding I am not responsible for my son's life or his choices. Yes, it was possible I had an influence on his life growing up and I may offer some influence on his path to recovery; but, ultimately, I came to understand this was his life and his journey. What he needed most from me was a healthy dad. He didn't need me to try to fix things out of guilt or shame, he needed me at my best, if and when he needed me at all.

Once I started managing my emotions differently I started being the Dad he needed me to be, not the Dad I thought I needed to be. Now, relapse was not a personal setback to me, but a struggle for my son. I could come to my son in these situations with my love and commitment, to offer my encouragement and support, but, most importantly, giving him the space to learn and grow in the struggle.

This was a powerful behavioral change for both of us.

Mile 30

Trauma is not the event itself, it is our response to the experience of the event which defines and quantifies our trauma.

There are many contributing factors which can trigger substance use disorder in an individual. Many of the more recent studies indicate there is a high correlation between addiction and trauma. Trauma takes many forms. Most people identify trauma with extreme trauma experiences such as violence or death in the family, physical or sexual abuse, drug use in the home, or a family member in jail. Extreme trauma is not the only form of trauma linked to substance use disorder.

Personal trauma is another form of trauma. Examples of personal trauma are related to a person's experiences with verbal and physical abuse, self-perception or bullying, or environment experiences, such a moving, changing schools, divorce, etc.

To help identify trauma on another level, trauma research expert, Nadine Harris-Burke shares some examples in socio-economic terms. In urban areas, trauma is violence, jail, drugs and other related experiences. In poor rural areas trauma is experienced through prolonged poverty, interrupted education, and high rates of transiency. In affluent areas, trauma can be experienced through physical and emotional abuse, plus substance usage and dependency.

Understanding trauma and its impact involves recognizing it is not the event which produces trauma, rather it is the personal experience to the event which defines it. This helps explain why members of the same family can experience the same event and have entirely different behavioral responses to it. This also clarifies why parents often fail to recognize a traumatic experience of their child; the parent didn't experience the event as a traumatic to them, even though it was for their child. Additionally, if the child didn't share their traumatic experience with a parent, it may be less likely the parent was aware of the impact of the experience on their child.

Many parents, when first introduced to the concept of trauma, often respond that their children haven't experienced trauma.

This may be true in the sense that, to the parent, their child didn't experience a traumatic event. A traumatic experience can be completely dependent upon how an experience impacted an individual, not necessarily the event itself.

Trauma is personal, relating directly to how an individual experienced an event. Also, children rarely share with their parents the struggles they experience at school, so it might be difficult for them to know about their child's trauma unless made aware of it. In schools, bullying, physical intimidation, and verbal abuse could easily become traumatic experiences completely dependent upon how that experience impacted the individual, not what the experience was. As a result, traumatic events can become internalized and the impact of them manifest themselves in other ways, including but not limited to substance use disorder.

As we seek to improve our approach to the treatment of substance use disorder, much can be gained from a better appreciation for the relationship between trauma and the impact on the brain. Because we have substantial evidence of scientific study to support a correlation between trauma and addiction, we are now better positioned to treat substance use disorder as a brain disorder.

Author Maia Szalavitz, in her book *Unbroken Brain*, says "in the context of addiction...the more discomfort, distress, trauma, and pain we feel – whether due to over reaction to ordinary experience, under reaction to it, or normal reaction to traumatic experience – the greater the risk." When we hear people talking about their drug of choice in terms like "numbing pain, escaping the pain, or trying to find ways to feel better." These are all references to someone who has experienced trauma and have become addicted to a substance, behavior, or activity as a resource for managing the struggle of the experience.

This explains why effective treatment modalities are going beyond teaching and reinforcing abstinence in recovery. Effective recovery has two components. The first is keeping the brain clear of mind altering substances. The second is treating the psychological component focused on trauma. It is important parents understand and seek out this treatment approach when searching for treatment facilities and recovery options.

Mile 31

Have you ever wondered why some people simply seem to get stuck in life?

Those who are negatively addicted embrace a reality in their darkness that "this is as good at it gets." In that mindset they lose hope and settle in to the situation they are in rather than move out of it....Those who are positively addicted look at their life and say "there has got to be an answer." They spend their lives doing things that move them forward in pursuit of the answer. Positive Addiction, William Glasser

Have you struggled to understand why your child can't embrace their treatment or recovery program? I know I couldn't understand why my son would say things like, "it's not going to change anything" or "what difference will it make?" or "what's the sense?"

These are the words spoken by a person who has lost hope. Their perspective, their world, is one where; "this is as good as it gets". There is little to look forward to or believe in from their vantage point.

Try as we might, a person who has resigned themselves to this space of hopelessness, will only change their mind once they change their viewpoint. I spent a great deal of time reminding my son of all those who loved him, of the amazing gifts and talents he possesses, the impact he has on others in his life and so much more. Despite my affirmations, he couldn't accept it as his truth.

He was resigned to his reality that this is as good it gets.

Sadly, there is little we can do to force a change in perspective other than continuing to find ways for them to experience our love for them and to avoid engaging in conversations which points to loss, disappointment, or failure, as these only feed the loss of hope mindset.

Loss of hope can also become a parent or loved one's view. The dramatic shift in our own mindset as addiction's chaos seems to have taken permanent residence in our lives, often causes parents to make the same declaration; "It's never going to get any better than this."

Loss of hope can impact a parent or loved one's life in a similar fashion. Once we resign ourselves to the permanency of this addiction situation, then depression, substance use, health issues, broken relationships can all become part of a resignation to a life of hopelessness. Parents and loved ones are encouraged to continue to engage in activities, programs, and behaviors which keep them on the path of believing there is an answer. Loss of hope is detrimental to anyone who experiences it. Activities which push forward in search of an answer instill hope in us, as our minds and bodies are positively stimulated and the head trash in our minds get cleared out, if for a moment. Engaging in these activities provide parents and loved ones with the energy, the space, and the capacity to take a fresh look at the struggle on a regular basis. It is difficult to get stuck when we're moving.

Mile 32

It is impossible to stop feeling what you are feeling or completely interrupt your thoughts.

You can learn to better manage your feelings, but it is virtually impossible to completely ignore hem or will them away. However, it is possible to minimize our dwelling on them or repeatedly expressing them outwardly. In the heat of an emotionally charged moment, controlling our outbursts can often be a challenging exercise. Managing feeling and opinions involves learning to acknowledge them, release them, and move forward without having them do much harm to ourselves or others.

In my experiences with parents and children in substance use disorder conflicts, most relationship damage is done when emotions escalate, a battle ensues, regrettable words are shared, or a reactive, angry decision is made. The best time to make and share critical decisions or engage in difficult conversations is not when emotions or tempers are highly charged. They are best accomplished in a quiet, rational setting, where what needs to be conveyed occurs in a less emotional charged environment.

I recognize it can be difficult to create these environments, or maximize them, when a child is actively in their addiction. However, I have found that parents make the best decisions when they create a quiet space to organize their thoughts and develop a rational approach to the issue.

While their child may never be in a perfect emotional state to have a rational conversation, quiet time planning and intentional timing helps reduce the stresses which come from reactive, agitated, emotional conversations.

When there is no relief from highly stressed situations, it becomes more and more difficult to navigate a life around them. In the highly charged emotional climate of addiction's chaos, detachment is a healthy and necessary behavior.

Detachment facilitates a healthy separation from toxic or stressful environments or situations.

Detaching is not an escape.

It a process by which you remove yourself emotionally and physically from a situation, in full awareness you will need to return to deal with it eventually. Detachment allows you to distance yourself from the chaos and reflect from a place of relative peace and clarity to organize your thoughts and re-connect with your rational, logical side.

Escape, unlike detachment, is akin to running away, to permanently avoid the situation, if possible. Escaping usually means the issue or problem will not be dealt with; or, is being assigned to someone else to manage, whether they're ready or not.

Escape provides little permanent relief as the issue is still present, it hasn't gone away. Escape simply means, I can no longer deal with it and I am going to avoid dealing with it, if possible. Unfortunately, there is no progress, healing, or resolution in escaping. It is just means that in the behavior of avoidance, I am hoping that somehow it will take care of itself. Rarely, especially in relationships does this result in a positive, effective, favorable long-term outcome.

Detachment represents a healthy time out.

Detachment is the process of discovering how to respond to a situation from a place of balanced emotion and logic. Detachment releases one from investing in a specific outcome, to the extent it is seen as right or wrong, winning or losing.

Detachment allows us the space to learn from the outcomes of our decisions, to assess the merits and failings of all options, and move forward, empowered by more information and wisdom. Through detachment, there is often a balanced approach in the decision-making process and a tempered response to the outcome and future strategies.

Mile 33

The wonderful gift discovered in the meditative activities of my bike rides, is the being able to observe my thoughts and emotions.

These observations provided me a period of healthy, logical reflection away from the chaos and the confusion.

On my bike, these periods of meditative release, thoughts and feelings come and go, just like the scenery on the side of the road routinely changes. There is no immediate need to react or rush to decide. This is the gift of meditation, the act of detaching. It helps put me in a quieter place to qualify all thoughts or emotions as good or bad, useful or not useful, or just letting them be what they are in the moment.

Stepping back and engaging someone from a place of detachment, from a place of peace, from a place of clarity, with a clear and intended purpose, increases the likelihood that your message is going to be clearer and better defined. It also improves the likelihood your message will be shared in an emotion-appropriate moment, thus minimizing the potential for highly charged emotional responses.

Bringing clarity, peace, and control into a sensitive situation changes the entire dynamic in a positive, productive, and powerful manner. Engaging in healthy dialogue in the appropriate moment provides the distinction between responding to the situation instead of reacting to it. For parents who are in their child's substance use disorder battle, detachment is often the first casualty. Parents can become so intensely focused on defining the outcome, obtaining the desired results, tracking progress and logging setbacks, they don't realize there is no longer a healthy separation from the chaos in their child's life and the parent's lives.

Crossing or having these blurred lines is usually where most of the trouble really begins. This is often where parents lose control in so many ways. They lose control of their lives because the addiction recovery battle becomes their life.

They lose control of their relationships because they don't have time for anyone else, but their child and themselves, on this full-time campaign. They lose control of their emotions as they have no capacity for releasing their emotional pain or recharging themselves. They lose control of their health because everything not relating to addiction including eating, working out, sleeping, are lesser priorities. They lose control to their obsession at incredibly high physical, emotional, and psychological costs.

Detachment helps to identify and engage in meditative releases from the chaos. Whether it is biking, hiking, running, walking, drawing, journaling, yoga or something else, healthy meditative detachment needs to be a component of parents' daily routine.

Over time, parents can get so far into their child's addiction recovery journey they don't realize the extent to which they are bringing their own broken toxicity into the situation. Instead, they end up hurting more than they are helping. They begin to interrupt their child's progress by getting in the way of their child's needs, and in some cases making things worse. When there is no detachment, perspective is lost. Nothing is more critical to a highly charged emotional environment than healthy balance and perspective. If the parents can't provide this resource, who will?

Recommended: *Full Catastrophe Living* written by Jon Kabat-Zinn

Mile 34

Over the course of your addiction journey, you will have, or have had, many difficult and challenging conversations with your children. Whether these conversations took place in the heat of battle or in a more tranquil moment, the words you choose and the tone you use linger in ways you may not realize.

When you share with someone the gift of your *unconditional* love, you are committing that no matter what they've done, who they've become, or how they are living – you love them. Love is selfless, generous, kind, patient, understanding, eternal, and, most of all, it is unconditional.

I remember listening to the story of a good friend, who was in the middle of the worst aspects of her crystal meth addiction. Somehow her mom searched her out and found her in this wasteland of a hotel room. She was shocked her mom even found her.

All her mom desired was to see her daughter. As she tells this story of this meeting with her mom, the only part she truly remembers is her mom saying to her, *"I want you to know, I love you. I don't love this (looking at the visual mess of her life) but I love you!"*

She was blown away. Despite all she had done, where she was, and what she was doing, her mom simply looked at her and said, "*I love you!*" That was the day this woman began her road to recovery. She was moved by that powerful exchange — knowing her mom loved her no matter what changed everything.

Nobody ever wants to disappoint someone we love or who loves us. Hearing a loved one share their disappointment in them is very traumatic.

A person battling an addiction is already struggling with an internal sense of failing, emptiness, guilt and loss. They do not enjoy their addiction, they are in constant battle with it, and it is difficult for them to find hope in the middle of their chaos. The last thing they need to hear from anyone is a hurtful reminder of how much they have failed those they love. It will never motivate, it will not build confidence and it doesn't help.

"I know. I remember the day my dad said he was disappointed in me. It is fresh in my mind, as though it was yesterday. It hurt me more than anything." This experience was shared by a young, single mom at a treatment facility. It was part of a conversation I was having with a group of around twenty young, single moms, in recovery.

When we were talking about words which had the most impact, positive or negative, "love" and "disappointment' were the two most popular. The reaction of all the women in the room to the word "disappointment" taught me this is the most painful, hurtful word a child can experience with their parent.

Mile 35

Your child does not need to be reminded of your disappointment.

Too often parents feel the need to remind, exonerate, or tell their children what they need to do to get out of their active addiction. It becomes part of the ongoing, routine dialogue to point to the chaos and remind them they need to do to clean up their lives. The truth is, children already know what they need to do. If they could, they would. No one chooses to remain addicted.

There are two forces behind their unwillingness to acknowledge your continued reminding. One is denial and the other is belief. In denial they are deflecting your truth in order to protect their truth. If they acknowledge what you are demanding and expecting of them, which is a change in their current lifestyle, they know the next step will be for you to expect them to take action to change it. They are not prepared or ready to change it. Instead, they deny your interpretation of their life as accurate or deflect your expectations to preserve something they may not like, but are not ready to change. In their twisted logic, it is easier to maintain in the place they are than to acknowledge where they are and be forced to do something about it. The simplest way to deflect this discussion is to live in denial and avoid the conversation or deflect your truth. Belief is the other emotion behind their unwillingness to respond to our calls to action.

Sometimes it is easier to remain in addiction than it is to believe recovery is possible. They are not choosing to use, they are choosing not to recover. Not because they want to use, but because they don't know how, or don't believe, they can recover successfully.

Berating a child because they are failing at recovery, only feeds the beast of shame, guilt and disappointment our children are already battling. Finding a way to love them and accept them, without demands and disappointment, shifts their experiences with you and helps them find hope within themselves, which is where recovery must emanate.

I have been blessed with many lessons and continue to receive education, encouragement, and insights from this incredible community of parents of children addicted to drugs. The one thing I have learned more than anything else is the only gift I can truly give my son at this point in his journey is the gift of *unconditional love* and *unrelenting hope* measured by my commitment of love and acceptance, even if he is in active addiction. I refuse to lose our connection. I remain committed to improving our relationship, even in the messiness of addiction.

Research has demonstrated that 70% of the people who have changed their destructive mental behaviors did so because of a connection with someone who inspired change.

Think about this, a meaningful connection inspiring change. In our relationships, our words and our behaviors matter. They matter not in the sense of parents demanding their child meets them where they are, or to their expectations, rather the parents, like my addicted friend, meet their children where their child is with a message of love and acceptance. This may be one of the most difficult activities to engage in, but it has proven to have an incredibly powerful impact on change.

Children with substance use disorder have enough of a load on their shoulders fighting their addiction battle, they don't need to be carrying the weight of a parents' expectations, disappointment, or approval. Please keep this in mind next time you get into the word game with your addicted loved one. What you say, how you live it out, makes a huge difference.

Mile 36

So my son is sitting outside my door in the pouring rain with nowhere to go. It is breaking my heart.... I am no good at this "tough love" thing. He's been here four months. I took him to detox twice and to rehab to which he left. Today he robbed me again. I told him not to come back. Now he's sitting outside saying he and has nowhere to go. What do I do? I can't take it anymore! ~ A mom sharing her personal agony.

It is extremely difficult to know what to do in these situations. As a parent, each of us want to take our child in, give them a hug, put them in dry clothes, and show our love for them. That is a normal and very appropriate response.

It is hard to adjust or alter the way we communicate with our children in response to the situation they are in. We do not want to punish them, we never want them to experience painful consequences as a result of the choices they make, and we certainly don't want to lose our child to their addiction driven mistakes.

If we protect them, make exceptions for them, shield them from outcomes they need to learn from – how can we possible expect them to change or alter their behaviors? If they know there are no consequences, only the threat of one, they will not be responsible for changing anything.

A child with substance use disorder puts parents in painfully difficult situations. They challenge us to do things we never would have imagined or believed possible. Their decisions hurt and confound us.

Their actions often confuse and threaten to destroy us. Eventually we are going to have to make some tough decisions if we are ever going to regain our sanity, take control of our life, and challenge our children to make their own choice and learn from their behaviors.

"I am struggling. My 22-year-old daughter has been on a path of addiction for about five years. I constantly teeter on whether to stop communication because of the heartbreak I experience when I see her in active addiction; or, buck up and pretend there isn't an elephant in the room named heroin and just see her. It's such a catch 22. I miss her so much, yet when I do see her I feel complete sorrow and pain. I don't know how to handle being an addict's mom." ~ HW

Mile 37

I couldn't stand it; knowing there was not one thing I could do about it and had zero power over his situation.

I finally decided he needed to experience my love for him even if he was using and I began interacting with him in the most "normal" manner possible. So, we started getting together and simply enjoy each other's presence.

What it accomplished was it allowed my son to experience my love for him without any of my judgement, criticism or disappointment. We would talk about what he wanted to talk about and enjoy each other's company as best we could.

Eventually, our time would wind down. In respectful recognition of the boundaries we had established, he would go on his way back to the life he was living and I to mine.

These interactions were powerful. Not only did my son experience my love for him in a safe environment, he realized there could be a road back to his family from his addiction. So many children get kicked out or cut off by their parents and family in a moment of anger, hurt or disappointment they fear they may never be able to receive their parents' love again.

It requires mindfulness to focus on meeting them where they are and offering them nothing but unconditional love; but, it is the greatest gift you can give them. It reminds them there is always hope.

The effort required to get there involves a willingness to accept the reality that you are meeting hem where they are, in a place of unconditional love and acceptance. Whatever anger, hurt, disappointment, or pain you are feeling needs to remain checked and under control. This would be a good time to meditate, journal, go for a long walk, go for a run, or ride your bike – my favorite.

It would also be a good time to celebrate what isn't lost – a connection with your child. It may not be the most ideal relationship or the one you desire most; but, find comfort in having created a space to be connected, to share your love, and to demonstrate your commitment to them, regardless of their circumstances. That is something few children experience enough of.

"Crying! So sad! Eleven years dealing with my child's addiction! First, clean then relapsing. All of this has torn me apart! Who am I anymore? So sad! So depressed! I feel guilty because I no longer have the faith I used to have that they will get clean and stay that way. I'm so, so broken! I go to meetings! I pray! Why does it never stay better?" ~ A mom dealing with addiction in her world

It is difficult to separate or detach from the chaos of our children's choices. As parents we spend much of our children's early lives loving, teaching, advising, encouraging, protecting, and fixing them. As our children get older, we worry about the choices they are making and the older our children get the bigger, riskier, and more terrifying the stakes become. Add the dynamic of a child battling an addiction and everything increases exponentially.

There comes a time when we, as parents, need to detach from our children. Their choices, actions, behaviors, outcomes, and consequences need to be theirs to choose, live, and experience. It is not healthy or productive to be that connected to their lives. They have their life and we have our own lives to live.

I know how this mom feels. I once was lost trying to save, cure, fix, guide, direct and control my son's choices and outcomes. It got to the point where every single action in his addiction driven life influenced and defined the next step or action in mine. I was officially out of control, co-dependent, and addicted to his addiction.

Mile 38

Once again, it was time for him to go.

"Watching someone you love, walk away at 6:30 in the morning, tired, hungry and knowing they are going back on the street is heartbreaking. As I looking out, seeing that depressed and tired expression on his face as he looked back at our house, tore me up inside. This is how it has to be..... What if there is no bottom? I thought this time home they would decide to seek help but it was not to be. I fear his bottom may be suicide one day. If that happens, will I be able to live with that?"

There comes a point in a parents' addiction journey when they realize they have no control over their child's decisions. This discovery is not limited to parents of children with addiction issues, it is every parents' reality. There comes a point as our children get older where we cannot tell them what to do, we can only advise them. Eventually, parents realize we cannot advise anymore, unless asked. The difference between a normal parental journey and one challenged by the continued presence of addiction, is the depth to which we experience our inability to influence the choices our children make.

While most parents live a life of natural concern and worry over the behaviors of their child, a parent in the addiction journey has a much higher level of angst. Their children are in a living battle for their lives, their soul, and their future.

We finally release them to their choices, only after we have resigned ourselves to the reality that there are limits to how much we can actually help them.

Parenting has never been easy. We want so much for our children that it is hard to watch them struggle, fail, fall down, or get lost. Being a parent is a lifetime commitment. There is never a time when once someone becomes a parent, they stop being a parent. Even when a child grows old, marries, and has children of their own – we are still parents.

Being a parent is not our only responsibility, though. Being a parent means that there are times where we must let our children find their path through discovery and experience – even if it is a dangerous one.

There comes a point where love, hope, and encouraging are going to have to be enough as we let them go to face the consequences, outcomes, and impact of their choices, their dreams, or their mistakes. It is not easy letting go.

It is even harder to let go of a child who is lost, hurting or sick. Regardless, it is their path, their journey and their life — they need to find it, follow it, and live it on their terms.

Along the way we can hope, pray, and offer encouragement and direction. If all goes according to our dream for them, they will return to us inspired, changed, and happy. That is what letting go is all about!

Mile 39

A new and different day.

Once we find ourselves in the middle of the storm, all we can think about is getting back to the place where it wasn't this hard or this painful.

"I just want something to feel like normal."

When we are deep in the struggle, it is hard to imagine anything positive emerging from that experience. You just want it to be over with.

At some point, every parent realizes there is no going back. Despite our desires to protect what is or what was, everything has been forever changed. While at first, you may grieve the change, hopefully, you will begin to see beyond the pain and discover what other opportunities are out there.

Adversity teaches us the lessons we are not willing to teach ourselves.

There is often a significant growth opportunity in every adversity. The more difficult the journey, the more profound the experience.

Any parent's substance use disorder journey is a particularly gripping and emotional one. My son's addiction was and is the greatest individual struggle of my life. It also was and continues to be the greatest gift in my life.

- It became a gift the minute I made the decision I was not going to try to control the problem or be able to change the person with the problem.
- It became a gift the moment I decided to change how I dealt with, responded to, and experienced the outcomes of my son's addiction.
- It became a gift when I declared it as his addiction, not mine.

Your child's addiction has changed you.

It has taken you from a place where your dreams for your life and your child's life became interrupted by a monster. It seized control of your world and turned it upside down. It took everything you believed and understood about love, trust, and hope and tore it apart. Now, it has taken over control of your life.

You have been changed, seemingly for the worse. It is now time to be changed for the better. Breaking free from the grip of addiction means you cannot let the addiction take over your life, your priorities, your behaviors, and your expectations for someone else. You must set healthy boundaries, clearly define your rules, and take care of yourself. Without it, the addiction owns you, too.

Battling the addiction that exists in another person is a fruitless effort. The addiction is in control of your loved one and will be stopped when your loved one makes that determination to engage in the fight to reclaim control of their life.

You are not the one with the addiction. You can choose to say "no" to that addiction at any time. If you haven't it is likely because you feel a sense of responsibility for helping that loved one fulfill the hopes and dreams you have for them. That is noble, honorable, and a wonderful, loving commitment; but, you cannot go down with the ship. In doing so, the addiction claims two lives. There are others who need you, love you, depend on you, and are blessed by your presence when you are on your game, and in your own lane.

Mile 40

You cannot beat the monster which exists within another person.

As long as you are fighting their beast, you are giving it power to break you down and destroy you, as well – one painful, hurtful lesson after another. You have been changed. You are forever changed. This change can take on a powerful and impactful tone the day you wake-up and embrace living an addiction free life.

Addiction free means taking control of your life, not fighting to be in control of someone else's. You will be positively transformed the moment you say, I can't live like this anymore, and do exactly what you know you need to do to reclaim your life.

You will never be free of the addiction as long as your loved one suffers with their disorder; but, being addiction free means that addiction cannot and will not destroy you along the way. As you struggle with difficult, challenging adversity in your life, such as the addiction and substance abuse in your family:

- **Trust in your ability to weather the storm**. While you have never been through something this difficult before, you have experienced previous struggles and you maneuvered through them. This may be bigger, more difficult; but, the process is no different. You will get through it.

- **Look for guidance and direction from those who you can trust with your journey.** This was the breakthrough step for me. I worked hard at trying to find my way, on my own. Once I found others I could honestly share my struggles with, my perspective and responses completely changed. I learned to embrace the journey in a more profound way because I knew I was not alone and I had a great support team working with me.
- **Embrace the growth opportunities which present itself.** This is not to say there is something "wrong" with you; but, the growth lesson only comes when you put yourself in a position to challenge the way you have always done things, examine how you can live and do them differently, understand why, and commit to the change.
- As you move through the chaos created by this experience, celebrate how far you've come from where you were when this crisis began. Being fixated only on the objective of surviving the storm is exhausting. Give yourself continuous, little energy boosts by acknowledging every step forward, ever new mile covered.

There is tremendous opportunity for you to grow, evolve, and celebrate the hidden insights in this difficult journey. It is a battle you didn't sign-up for or volunteer to be part of. It is your battle just the same. I encourage you to fight the battle for your life, it is the most important battle out there. There is a gift in the outcome and, it is getting your life back on track.

Mile 41

Focus on what you can control, letting go of what you simply can't control.

Parental protection of their young children is to be expected, it's necessary. As children mature, we as parents have the expectation that they will becoming ever more responsible in their decisions and with their choices. If a parent does not adjust to these development changes an over-protective stance can become unhealthy and hinder independence and self-confidence in the child.

Parenting a child with substance use disorder blurs these lines even more, as it is very hard for parents to understand their children are not completely helpless and there are some things they need to figure out and learn on their own.

I was there, playing out the role of a parent determined to protect their child. I drove my son to meetings, to drug tests, to work, to his probation officer meetings and wrote letters to judges. Any and all opportunities I had to protect my son, help minimize the impact of his addiction on his life and do everything in my power to get him to recover, I did. Sadly, little changed in this scenario until I changed. I stopped doing the work and turned it over to him.

The only way to really help your child discover a path to their recovery is to empower them to be responsible for their lives and decisions, allowing them to feel the impact of the choices they make.

You only have control of two things, your attitude and your effort.

Trying to control things which are beyond my control is one of my bad habits. Control is an elusive reality. The more I fight to maintain control of anything, the more I discover I never really had control in the first place.

Here is what I have learned about control and my inability to control what isn't mine to control:

- People will do things we just don't understand, including stuff that hurts themselves and you;
- Despite your best efforts to stop, prevent, and protect, this happens anyway;
- The greater your fear of the worst outcome, the stronger your desire to control a better one;
- Even though you know you have no control, you are still surprised and hurt when, despite your best efforts, your inability to be in control is often confirmed;
- When you let go of what you can't control, something still draws you back in, and you are often reminded of the reasons why you intended to let go afterward;
- Every time you fail to control the uncontrollable, you experience a sense of failure and disappointment;
- Your desire to control kicks in high gear when fear is at its highest; or a lack of trust is at its lowest;
- Taking control over someone else's responsibilities is a burden to you and an insult to them;
- Even when committing to complete surrender, you still find yourself defining outcomes, results, and actions, in an effort to influence the outcome you desire;
- Control is a by-product of fear, doubt, worry, and distrust.

I wish I could say I have discovered and consistently applied my secret formula for surrendering control. I haven't, yet. Even though I have made tremendous improvements, it is a continuous, intentional work in progress. I have become much more cognizant of those moments where I am allowing strong emotional states to drive my behaviors and to notice on a more regular basis when I slip off the rails and back into the comfort of a parent take-control mode. Stepping back and affording myself the time to figure out what is working and what is clearly not is making a positive difference. Now, like so many other things in life, I practice, practice, practice.

Life is finding its pace once again, and that is something that offers much relief.

Mile 42

On my Route 66 cycling trip, I had a most memorable experience passing through Litchfield, IL.

It was lunchtime as I passed through the center of town when I noticed a car in the far-left lane slowly heading in the other direction toward me.

As I got close, a woman waved at me, leaned out her window and shouted; "Are you Dave?" I acknowledged with a wave and watched her make a U-turn, pass me, and park her car about a half-mile down the road.

It turned out she had seen the news story about the bike trip on the St. Louis television station and had been watching for me all morning.

When she saw my support vehicle which had been riding ahead of me pass by, she jumped in her car to find and meet me. When we stopped to talk, this mom had one burning question. Her son had been in long-term recovery for about six months and she wanted to know what she could do to help him stay on this path. She was struggling to manage her fears about potential relapse by discovering what she could do to help control or manage his sustained recovery. While I offered her some helpful tips and suggestions for loving him and encouraging him, I reminded her she has no control over his recovery. While she was hoping for a miracle answer, she knew this was correct. We talked more about how she could care for herself, love her son where he was, and ideas for encouraging and supporting her son without taking over his recovery.

I would have loved to give this mom a more definitive solution or plan for controlling the outcomes we desire in others, the truth is we can only control ourselves, manage how we care for ourselves and be a healthy resource for our children when they ask us for help.

Mile 43

The words we choose to use.

As I began to become more aware of my behaviors with my son, I also began to focus on my dialogue, the words I used with him.

Early in my journey with my son's addiction, much of what I focused on were related around checking up on him, encouraging him, and telling him what my strategies were in relation to where he was in life. The tone of our conversation, to me, seemed healthy and productive. After all, I was demonstrating sincere concern in helping move him from where he was to where he needed to be. It seems appropriate and reasonable, until I look closely and honestly what is behind these behaviors:

- **Checking up on him**: Repeatedly, checking in is a slippery slope. If I am checking in to see how he's doing or feeling, this can be productive. But, if checking in involves going through his list of responsibilities, i.e., work, meetings, other obligations, I have crossed the line into monitoring, managing his behaviors. This represents a shift from being a loving concerned parent and to being a controlling parent.
- **Encouraging him**: Encouraging my son isn't always seen as encouragement to him. Sometimes encouraging my son, helping him believe he can do it, unintentionally calls attention to the reality that he hasn't done it, yet. Encouragement can have a

negative effect on our children. We believe we are helping them believe in their ability, when they are struggling with this belief and only see our encouragement as a reminder of where they are falling short on their failed journey, not in experiencing or hearing our belief in their ability to succeed.

- **Telling him what I think he needs to do**: Parents are the masters of unsolicited opinions. I know I was. We love telling our children what they need to do in regard to almost everything in their life. While we believe we are giving great advice and offering incredible wisdom and insight, our children hear otherwise. Once again, we are telling them what we want of them, without understanding what they want or need from us. The same is true with my son's interactions with me. He already knows what he needs to do in relation to his addiction. The success model to recovery never changes. *He isn't struggling with knowing it, he is struggling with doing it.* This is not a strategy issue, it is a mental disorder issue stemming from the addiction.

Take note of the perspective or point of view in these three actions. My conversation is about me: what I see, what I want, what I believe, and what I expect. I am doing what I think I need to do to be the parent I need to be. I am not engaging him in a place where I am discovering how he is doing and what he needs from me.

I am telling him, judging him, criticizing him, and not listening to him.

I am projecting my demands, needs, and expectations on him without having any understanding of where he is, what he is struggling with, what he needs from me or how I can help, if he asks. This awareness has resulted in a powerful shift in our dialogue and in our relationship. I have focused on eliminating all dialogue which project judgement, criticism or condemnation. Instead I replaced it with love, acceptance, and empathy. I avoid talking about treatment, recovery, work, or probation unless he brings them up. I don't ask about his future plans for his life or where he envisions on going from here, unless he opens the door. And, in all situations, I avoid telling him what I think, see or believe unless he asks me. Instead I listen, I engage, and I encourage him to share with me where he is and what is going on in his life.

This is a very difficult exercise. This was my most challenging shift. This was a critical step in releasing my son from me.

Mile 44

What our children need is a place to be safe, to experience love, and sort out their path one step at a time.

Many parents believe their children don't care what they have done or who they hurt on their addiction journey. Nothing could be further from the truth.

According to my son, they are aware of the pain they are causing, they just cannot help it. And, while they feel the hurt in their choices, their addiction will not let them avoid bad choices.

Children in addiction are manipulative, conniving, and incredibly selfish. All they want is their drug. How we engage our children, the conversations we have with them, even in active addiction, has tremendous healing, transformational power.

Over the course of this book, as I share my perspectives from my journey with my son, there has been a consistent theme – love your children where they are, for who they are.

How we communicate with them, the words we choose, the words we use, are a critical piece in this process.

When our children experience love, acceptance, empathy in their engagements with their parents, it leaves a mark on them. Those behaviors resonate, even if we don't experience the immediate results we desire from them.

Mile 45

Once something takes a turn for the worst, our emotional system goes into overdrive and we begin looking for ways to protect ourselves.

This is a natural process, as the limbic system in our brain is hardwired to sense and protect us from danger. Conflict and threats signal danger and our brain responds by helping define how we to respond to protect ourselves. The limbic system senses a threat and uses a combination of logic and emotion to help us decide whether to fight, flee, or freeze. This helps explain why, in the face of a chaotic situation, our minds and emotions seem to be racing out of control. It is our brain helping us define how to best respond to the situation.

Humility, vulnerability and trust are not behaviors readily used to describe or define protecting ourselves. The opposite behaviors of ego, protectiveness, and doubt or mistrust are easily associated as behaviors relied on for protection or where someone might find safety or security.

The problem with these protective behaviors in the long-term is there is no room for healing after the immediate danger or threat has passed. Trauma stimulates our limbic system in much the same way these protective behaviors do. Protective behaviors, a stimulated limbic system, help protect us from threats. An overstimulated limbic system, one that is continually being triggered, is not good for us physiologically or psychologically. It impacts cognitive learning, leads to stress related health issues and can even shorten our life. Operating in protection mode through our ego, distrust, and defensiveness has similar impacts on our overall health.

Even though humility and vulnerability cannot protect us, they are a valuable resource to help us heal and grow. When we allow ourselves to stay stuck in protection mode, there is little opportunity to heal from what hurts or scares us. This self-protective behavior can keep us stuck in a place of fear and has tremendous impact on our physical and mental health, our relationships, and our personal development and growth.

In this journey, I have learned a great deal about the healing and developmental power in vulnerability, authenticity, and trust. This was not an easy process. It was incredibly difficult for me to engage in, but it provided an incredible shift which healed me in very powerful ways.

Vulnerability means trusting someone with who we are, where we are. Vulnerability requires being real with ourselves and with others. Vulnerability or transparency is like removing the mask I was wearing to convince others how strong and capable I desired to be seen as, without revealing where or how I was struggling.

It is difficult to take off the mask. Our mask provides us protection from others, it hides our weaknesses, and helps maintain our capable persona. Unfortunately, it also prevents us from receiving the support, love, and encouragement we so desperately need from others, especially those who deserve our trust.

Mile 46

Right, Good, Control, Win!

For most of my life, and especially when I was struggling with my son's addiction, the bricks I used to build and maintain my protective wall were defined by these four words.

It was a conversation with a life coach who pointed this out to me. When she shared this perspective about how I manage my life in times of adversity, I was blown away. It was one of those "Wow!" experiences.

What I learned in the exchange was I was defining success, accomplishment, and safety or protection by these words. I had to be right, I had to be in control, I had to be good, and I had to win.

As I reflected on the struggles I was having as a parent in this very chaotic period, my mindset placed me in an untenable position. I had to make the right decisions, I was fighting to control the situation, I didn't want to be a bad parent, and I had to win the battle over my son's addiction at all costs. This placed me in a very unhealthy position. I was dealing with a situation with my son where the right decision isn't always known, where I had little control, things didn't always end up in a good place, and I was fighting a battle which was not mine to win. Worse, all the barriers I had constructed in the form of these four words, didn't really create a great deal of space for others to climb the wall of defense to help or support me. I was in this battle on my own, by my own doing.

Once I came to discover the impact these four words were having on me, I started to focus on recognizing when I would take action reflective of right, good, control, and win. I found myself shifting from these self-reliant drivers and connecting with others who were providing encouragement and guidance. I no longer was hunkering down in this self-protective battle of survival.

Mile 47

I had to find a way to protect myself from more emotional pain.

My behaviors and decisions were defined by *being right, being good, being in control, and winning.* This best describes how I have historically maneuvered, or powered through, most of the difficult situations in my life.

While these activities enabled me to be externally strong, internally I remained broken and isolated or alone. They also prevented anyone reaching me, as my rules for engagement required others to **be *wrong, be bad, cede control, or lose.*** Under these conditions, there isn't much room for receiving the power of love or guidance from others. This operating environment allowed me to be in complete control of the process and the outcome, unable or unwilling to admit I needed help (there's that control word, again). It didn't leave much room for humility, vulnerability, trust or love.

Only when I began to admit I needed the support of others and start asking for help and assistance from those I could trust, did I really heal and grow in my adversities. This shift has made and continues to make an enormous difference in my life, especially as I heal and grow on my addiction journey.

It takes many caring, engaged others to successfully tackle a family crisis like addiction. It takes people working together authentically to lift each other up, love each other, encourage one another, and be accountable to each other.

Vulnerability and trust are critical behaviors as our ability to be an effective resource partner in this chaos requires everyone to be honest and real. It requires taking off the mask of self-protection and being honest about our pain and confusion in the situation. When we put up protective barriers we prevent and block others from helping us. Putting our protection-oriented behaviors in control sends a message to our most reliable, capable resources, I don't trust you with me.

This leads to an interesting relationship conundrum:

If I can't trust you with me, how can you trust me with you?

The inability to trust, be authentic, or embrace humility is what divides loved ones and parents in families touched by substance use disorder. Parents often take up their battle stations to fight their own personal, internal battles, resulting in the loved one left to struggle with their addiction n isolation from a parents' self-protection related behaviors. This occurs with parents' inability to collaborate, with being vulnerable or engaging in safe conversations to work through the struggle together. Instead their conversations and behaviors are driven by protection and safety, around being right, being in control, winning, and not being bad.

This behavior divides parents and isolates them as they unilaterally, independently respond to the issue, rather than trust their partner with what scares, terrifies and frustrates them. In the end, this divide allows the child to prey on the brokenness in the parental dynamic which often leads to more chaos and division, and perpetuates a vicious and completely avoidable cycle.

Once I made the shift from right, good, control, and winning, there were many transitive activities and outcomes. Recognizing when these behaviors would start to take over marked the beginning of my shift. Awareness is always the primary step toward change. Being aware of the times when I would begin to take over (control), keep score (winning), measure correctness (good), or focus on acceptance (right) helped me be more cognizant of when and why I was doing it.

This shift not only benefitted me in how I began to respond to the challenges of my son's addiction, it also helped in my interactions with my wife. Early on in this journey, I made all the decisions, defined the response to issues, and pretty much operated in my own little autocratic bubble. I didn't really collaborate or engage my wife for her opinions, perspectives, and concerns. Instead, I got in an unhealthy pattern of simply reporting to her what "we" were going to next or how "we" were going to handle the current crisis before us.

A big driver behind these behaviors were my own fears and concerns about making a mistake, a bad decision or making things worse. My self-protecting behaviors were preventing me from seeking support, guidance, or help from someone who had as much invested in my son's recovery as I did. As a result, I shut his mom, my wife, out of the thought process.

Once I began to engage my wife in these conversations, allowed myself to be more vulnerable and open, it provided both of us the ability to learn from each other, to gain broader perspective and begin to share what we were experiencing and feeling on this journey. Even if it was a simple as soliciting her opinion as to "what do we do now?" provided a significant shift in our conversations and decisions regarding my son's behaviors and challenges.

Mile 48

There was a clear pattern to my self-protection triggers.

As soon as I became uncomfortable with where something was headed or what I may be called upon to do or say, I found myself analyzing my options to make myself more comfortable and safe.

Defaulting to my old behaviors allowed me to be safe, to be protected; but they weren't allowing me to be real or authentic or trust others with who I was and where I was in the situation.

I needed guidance and direction, but I wasn't willing to admit it enough to ask for help or guidance without revealing my vulnerable, authentic side. Embracing my fears allowed me to be safe, even though I wasn't accomplishing anything other than being temporarily protected from the truth about me.

What I worked on and continue to work on, is to step out of my place of fear and self-protection into being real with those around me. It has encouraged me to admit I am uncomfortable, I don't know how to respond to this, and I really could use a word of encouragement or advice from someone who knows me and my struggle.

This was, and is, a big healing, helpful leap. The more I engaged in being authentic and trusting, the more I connected with others who were better equipped to support and love me. They trusted me because I was being real.

Those around me connected with me in very powerful ways. The collaboration of ideas and solutions in our individual struggles were profound. I have learned to grow and more comfortably, confidently shift into this space because I have more experience with the incredible gifts vulnerability and trust offer.

Wherever you are on your journey, whatever fears, worries and doubts are getting in the way of your making better decisions with your child or preventing you from healing and growing in the process, find someone you can trust with your truth. Being truly vulnerability is very hard at first, but you will discover there is tremendous strength which comes from trusting someone with you.

Mile 49

It usually doesn't take long before parents get sideways with each other when dealing with their child and substance use disorder.

Parents have different ways of responding to their child's situation pertaining to drug use. As they are dealing with a highly emotional, stressful issue, it is natural for parents to get at odds with each other over the best way forward.

There are ways to minimize the divide or avoid it completely.

As shared earlier, trust and vulnerability are critical components in a collaborative, nurturing, and problem-solving environment. This is a requisite component of team parenting, as well. Let's examine some mindsets associated with each parent and where they usually are coming from: Mom: A healer, a nurturer. Wants to protect and save. Dad: A fixer. A problem solver. Wants to step in, take care of the problem, and move on.

When a child struggles with substance use disorder, often the mom takes on the role of caregiver, focusing on providing love, comfort, support, and assistance. Often times, Mom can cross the line into doing more than what is healthy or helpful. This is not to criticize, but to point out some of the potential pitfalls when operating with a particular and predominately nurturing mindset.

In contrast to the same situation, Dad tries to fix it. He steps in and applies a strategy to solve and fix the presenting problem. With substance use disorder, there isn't always a quick, simple or easy fix, which often confounds and frustrates those parents who are operating in that chosen mindset. After several failed attempts and repeated frustration, the pattern is for the logically driven parent to detach and extricate themselves from the problem.

Part of their exit strategy involves laying down some very hard boundaries and rules for the family to follow, while they move to a safe distance away from the chaos.

Recognizing these behavioral scenarios are broad generalizations and may seem inflammatory, but, they serve to point to trends I have witnessed often in the parental dynamic. It helps to point to these trending patterns to better understand the source of the conflict which often get in the way of parents working together.

A balanced approach stemming from a complimentary blend of these potentially conflictive behaviors makes all the difference in facilitating a team-oriented approach for dealing with the issue of substance abuse and substance use disorder in the family. The components of this interaction includes healthy boundaries, continuous and open communication, an educational commitment, and unconditional love.

When a commitment to teamwork, collaboration, and sustained communication and education fail, one partner may isolate to an unhealthy space, while the other is left alone while maneuvering around their spouse's retreating, angry directives.

This does not work! Moms and Dads, you are capable of being and doing so much more. Please allow me the space to encourage you to see yourself in the difficult space in a different manner.

Dads, your family needs you.

A house divided falls and addiction, by its very nature, is the divisive disrupter. Become engaged in learning more about substance use disorder, reach out and find support, while humbly, vulnerably ask for help.

Your child's addiction is not simply a problem to solve. You and your family are embarking on a new road of discovery and it needs a leader to guide them through it. Navigating this journey is best accomplished when both parents engage and walk this out together. Drop the negative talk, drop any need to blame, and shame.

Meet this challenge, do not give up or give in or walk away from those who need you the most, your partner and your other children, and family members.

Mile 50

Do not allow your child's addiction struggles to drive a wedge between you and your spouse.

Your spouse needs a partner who can be counted on, to lean on. Be that partner. Solving the substance abuse problem in your family isn't a responsibility any parent needs to bear alone.

1. Begin by engaging in open, honest conversations about what is happening, how it is impacting everyone, what your options are and agree on how you both are going to respond to it. Note the key words in the process: collaboration, conversation and agreement.

2. Be actively involved with your spouse and partner with each other on the learning curve. Attend educational programs and events together. Read educational books and articles together. Discuss and share what you both have learned and discovered together.

3. Learn all you can about the actual daily life of your child, whether they are using or not, in recovery or not. Listen to them. Let them share without your interrupting or demanding. Seek to understand their journey and their experiences, rather than go on a quest to simply fix the problem as you understand it to be.

There was a time, long before I learned of my son's heroin addiction, when my wife shared some information with me regarding my son's issue with prescription medication. I was busy with other things, figured she had it handled, and paid little attention to it.

She didn't really ask for help. But, there was likely a reason she told me. I missed out on the opportunity to support her and my son. I did not engage, I did not understand, I did not participate. It was a mistake. Years later, we ended up on a longer more challenging journey which may have been avoidable if I had engaged appropriately when I first had the opportunity. Either way, this memory serves as a reminder to be more sensitive to opportunities to support my spouse and my children when "little issues" arise.

4. Keep exploring for healthy solutions until balance and peace in your home has been restored. There is no need to be right, to assign blame or to point to failure in this process. In fact, you may even end up adjusting your expectations for peace and balance as you navigate the struggles your family is working through. The best approach is to learn from your decisions, define what could have been done differently or better, and always commit to discovering the next steps via agreement while honoring their implementation as one.

5. We all handle stress in many different ways. Know your style, your triggers, and the responses of all your family members to your behaviors. If they are healthy and productive, good. If they are not, examine how you can adjust or change them. At all times, do what you can to provide those you love, especially your spouse, a safe place to be heard, understood, and respected.

Mom and Dad need to work together.

When they don't, substance use disorder will manage and control the process. Any small, tiny crack in the parental armor is often pierced by guilt and manipulation. A very tight, united front working, in loving collaboration, is the best approach for helping your child.

As I shared earlier, there was a time when my wife and I didn't collaborate or communicate with each other, I simply made decisions based on what

I thought or believed was the best course of action. While I thought this was necessary and efficient, what I was did was isolate my wife from the educational and sharing process so critical for effective development and problem solving. While I was learning from my mistakes in relation to this journey, my wife wasn't on the same learning curve as me.

This stunted learning process affected us both, in different ways. First, my wife and I weren't sharing our discoveries and experiences with each other. We were responding to everything from our own perspectives and experiences, not in a position to benefit from the insights of the other.

Secondly, I had isolated my wife from the decision-making process. How we make decisions and our decision-making process provides a great deal of insight into what we know, believe, and understand about a situation. Sharing this insight with another helps them understand why a certain decision was made and provides a constructive place to assess the outcomes, including what could have been done differently and why. Not bringing my wife into the decision-making process prevented her from understanding my thought process and learning from it. Worse, it prevented me from learning from her about her thoughts, feelings and perspectives, all key components of a better decision-making process.

Once we got into the habit of sharing our perspectives and insights in our decision-making process, we learned more about our own individual experiences which enhanced our knowledge and awareness to the issues we were struggling with. More importantly, we became more comfortable and united about the decisions we were making together.

Mile 51

As a parent who has been on the addiction roller coaster, I can easily say fear was always the most present and strongest emotion.

I feared losing my son, I feared making bad decisions, I feared the worst-case scenario, I feared sharing my struggle with others, I even feared opening up about my fears. Fear was present in all my thoughts and had significant influence over many of my behaviors. Fear guided me to poor and unhealthy decisions as reason and logic were crippled by fear. Fear prevented me from engaging with others who were able to bring stability and emotional, physical health to my upside-down life.

Decisions made from a place of fear are often emotional reactions to complicated situations which rarely lead to the outcomes we desire as logic and reason have been minimized by the fear's intense presence.

Most parents operate in the delicate space between trust and fear. Healthy parenting behaviors involve looking beyond our fears of failing or of making a mistake, ultimately trusting our instinctual abilities to give our children what they need.

When parenting a child with an addiction, fear can easily overpower trust. Fear gets in our head, corrupts our thought process and influences our decisions, usually not for the better. Parents navigating their addiction odyssey have a very low tolerance for risk or failure. It is in this environment that fear reigns.

It took me a long time to become comfortable with the truth that love and trust is more powerful than fear. Releasing my fears and trusting in my love for my son, acknowledging there are no guaranteed outcomes in my choices, freed me to make more confident, time appropriate decisions.

Even as I moved more confidently into this truth, there were still moments where I panicked or hesitated in fear. Despite these fearful moments, I began to get better at trusting my instincts and letting them guide my decisions. It also allowed me to express my love for my son in ways that moved me beyond my fears, into a space of confident trust.

Love and fear are opposite behavioral emotions.

When fear defines our behaviors, love is overridden. When love defines our behaviors, fear is overcome. What facilitated this shift for me, was becoming more focused on trusting my instincts in relation to my love for my son and what I knew to be the best course of action at the time.

In this mindset, I would trust and listen to my "gut," not allowing my head trash, generated by fear, to corrupt my instinctive calls to act or respond.

I became more highly attuned to the initial pull in my heart on how to respond and didn't wait for my mind to assess the call to action and corrupt it with fear, doubt, or worry. This awareness propelled me forward – along yet another mile.

Mile 52

Simply releasing your fears and trusting your instincts sounds both vague and complicated.

It is, and it's not. Often when we are confronted with a situation, there is an immediate, almost reactive call for how to respond to it. It is our inner-self, applying all our experiences and self-awareness, providing us an insightful course of action. Nothing and no one knows us better than our inner-self. The initial internal guidance is the most insightful and accurate directive yet is one we often miss or override, especially in a fear-based mindset.

When we hear that inner voice tell us to just do something we often hesitate. We step back and think about that call to action in the context of other thoughts and options. Now, our brain gets into the process of managing the choices and the decision. Unfortunately, our brain is logically going through the assessment process, including our overriding emotions of fear, doubt and worry, to help define and justify our decisions. Too many times, that first instinct is rejected for a more logical, safer response.

How many times have you said, "I wish I had trusted my gut"?

Parents operating in a heightened state of personal emotional trauma, chaos and fear struggle to listen to their gut. Worn out, beaten down, and frustrated by continued failures and setbacks, many parents of children with substance use disorder don't know who or what to trust, including themselves.

I have been there, I know how disruptive our decisions are when made in this context. I am sharing this information to help other parents move away from this space and rediscover the confidence and peace which comes from trusting our instincts and releasing the fear.

I learned to trust my gut instincts and respond to that call to action as much as I possibly could. I got into a productive habit of listening to and trusting my instincts, knowing the source and power of this was based on a deep logical sense of what was best for me and for my son, and I trusted they were based on my profound love for my son.

As I learned to trust these instincts and make decisions and choices from this space, my decisions, their outcomes, and my emotional energy shifted and the results associated with them were different as well. This didn't mean the outcomes became better, because they didn't always go as I would have hoped. However, I found myself in a much calmer, trusting space relative to the chaotic environment that addiction can create, and learned to trust the outcomes from the decisions because I knew they were made from a much healthier, balanced place.

No longer operating out of fear, I was able to better connect with my son, even when things weren't going as I desired. Even when and if he was still using, we were able to interact and communicate in a civil, loving, healthy manner. We had conversations, not about addiction and recovery related stuff, but about things to which we shared mutual connection and joy over.

Once I moved away from a place of fear to a place of love and acceptance, it allowed my son to experience my love for him regardless of where he was on his journey.

Practicing love and acceptance completely shifted our relationship while providing him an opportunity to experience my love for him whenever we would connect. I knew I couldn't change or alter his behaviors, but I also knew he could experience my unconditional love for him at every turn.

I began to trust in the power of our love for one another. Regardless of what path he was on, experiencing my love for him at every turn served to remind him that no matter where he was on his journey, there is always a road home.

This approach is very different from the "tough love" theory of defensive, protective boundaries too often shared in parent organizations today.

When we kick our children out of the house, we unintentionally portray a message of conditional love. The action, by its descriptive term "kicked out", is a negative one. Attached to these actions are conditions to be met before one can be accepted. "Tough love" represents a negative, conditional love approach which is often overused, misapplied, and tragically misunderstood. And, is usually used in the context of a response which reflects a limited knowledge of the complexities of substance use disorder from all perspectives.

Mile 53

Love and acceptance reflects a balanced, healthy love approach.

My son is not be able to live with me because of the healthy boundaries we have established for everyone who lives in our house. It does not mean he can't visit, be a part of our family, or meet and converse with us.

I take every opportunity I can to meet with my son, pour love on him, and simply talk about life.

This is an opportunity for him to experience my love for him and my commitment to supporting him, when he is ready, on his recovery journey. There are no barriers to this connection, even in active addiction.

Below represents an example of a conversation I encourage parents to have with their child demonstrating what their unconditional love and commitment to them looks like. It shifts us from a place of fear to one of love and acceptance.

Making this shift will have a powerful impact on your relationship with your child:

"You have no idea how much I love you. In fact, my love for you is greater than anything I can offer. I know you are in the middle of a struggle. I know there is nothing I can do until you are ready to work through it. Know this,

because I love you as much as I do and crave nothing more than for you to find peace in your life, when you are ready to make a change, I will be there with you and we can walk this out together. I know it will take a lot for you to trust me with this commitment, but please remember this, when you are ready to take this journey with me, I will be there to take it with you. That is how much I love you."

Mile 54

There is a distinct difference between hearing and listening.

Most of our parental interactions involve a form of limited hearing, listening just long enough before we interrupt, correct, fix, or solve. Effective listening represents an entirely different behavior, involving an entirely different mindset and approach.

In the typical parenting world, we will listen to our child up the to that point where we feel compelled to jump in and remind them, correct them and tell them what our truth is. The problem is, we are telling them what we know, from our perspective, and not giving them what they need, based on their perspective and experiences. I call this behavior, selfishly telling. In this same space, we are also denying ourselves what we need most to help them. We are not obtaining the benefit of wisdom and perspective of understanding what they see, think, feel, experience, or struggle with. This information provides powerful insight critical for our ability to help them navigate their course in life.

Selfishly telling ends up projecting onto your child your frustrations with their choices, their substance abuse, and their addiction. Selfishly telling focuses on your experiences with their journey from your perspective, your expectations, your beliefs, and their world as you see it. Quite honestly, selfish telling serves to make parents feel like they are doing something because, in their desperation, they can't stand the thought of not being able to do anything. So they remind their child all the things they need to because they don't know how to make them do them. At least I was able to tell them.

I completely understand. I couldn't stand the path my son was on. I often felt as though I had to do or say something.

The longer he was on this path, the greater my frustration and the more obsessed I became about doing something about it. It was only until I realized how toxic these types of interactions were for me, my son, and our relationship did I stop doing it.

Mile 55

Consider your child's feelings during a verbal assault about what they need to do to fix their broken life.

What do they hear?

How do they feel?

What does it do for them, or how does it make them feel about themselves?

Do you really believe they don't know their life is out of control?

In a moment of complete honesty, my son told me I didn't need to remind him how messed up his life was, he was quite aware of it always.

Do you really think they don't know what they need to do to change it?

I have discovered in conversations with others who have navigated their life through substance use disorder, the question wasn't whether they knew what they needed to do, the challenge was believing or committing to doing it.

Do you honestly think that your continued harping on them is going to suddenly open their eyes and make them change their behaviors?

The shame people experience with their own failures and struggles with substance use disorder is enough. They do not and did not need others, especially those they love, reminding them of all their failures. They were struggling to find hope, letting them know your frustrations with their choices only shamed them more.

Think about what these types of interactions project onto your child, reminding them of their problems, their failures, and the things they need to do to fix their broken life. Imagine the impact these criticizing behaviors have on someone who is already feeling broken, isolated, alone and struggling to find their way out of their personal chaos. On top of it, imagine the pressure which comes from knowing how disappointed, frustrated or angry you are about their mess.

Are you really making things better, or are you feeding the adverse, toxic emotions of the addiction beast?

What if you switched your approach from selfishly telling, doing what you want to do to remind them where they need to be in your eyes, to Selfless Listening, creating a safe, protective space for them to openly share with you where they are, what they are going through, and their struggles and frustrations on their journey?

Selfless listening involves committing to listening to the person sharing, without an agenda, without fear, without interrupting or offering unsolicited opinions, without minimizing or dismissing the struggle, and without any judgement, criticism, or condemnation. It's a place where someone can safely, freely share the story of their journey, where they can be heard, understood, loved. Selfless listening is best exemplified in patience, empathy, love, and compassion.

It is difficult for a parent, desperate for their child to interrupt the habit of their destructive behaviors, to sit back and listen while repressing their desire to add their version of truth and reality to the dialogue. As difficult as it is, this exercise provides fresh, honest perspective for both parent and child.

Mile 56

Selfless listening is where one person encourages another to openly share what their world looks like and to explain their experiences.

It may even involve engaging in a healthy, open exchange about something other than their life, their struggle, their addiction and simply engage about books, school, work, friends, or the news of the day. Or find a way to laugh together, share a moment of the inconsequential.

Even if what is being shared makes no logical sense to the listener, it becomes the listener's responsibility to probe and inquire for more information, more insight to the point where the other person feels heard, understood, and supported. Being in a safe space to the point where they feel heard, understood, and supported is the entire objective of this behavior.

The advantages of selfless listening when interacting with a child in crisis are significant.

We only see understand from the limits of our perspective and perceptions. Without their sharing we cannot know what they're experiencing or going through.

Obtain a deeper sense of their issues, including what gets in the way of their success:

Up until now, we have them on our agenda and our plan for recovery, for life. How well do you understand what they need or where they desire to be? What if their goals, dreams, and desires are not what you think?

Facilitate a path for them to learn to trust you with their deep truths, instead of offering only "safe" information, complete BS, or something in between: Instead of getting mad at them for lying to you or holding back critical information, you now have an opportunity to create an environment where they can share real stuff without you flipping out or freaking out.

Engage in a process which models authentic communication from a place of love, trust, vulnerability and acceptance: Much of our own internal struggle is overcoming our own distrust of others to be authentic and engage in effective problem-solving interactions – selfless listening breaks the cycle.

If you want to inspire or guide someone to an incredible outcome or help them embrace change in their life, the place to start is by meeting them where they are. It is impossible to inspire change or instill a level of trust or confidence in what you are suggesting, if you don't understand what they believe they need to overcome to get there. Research has proven that becoming a trusted leader or facilitating change requires you listen first. People only trust those they feel understand them and know them. The same goes for your child. They won't be able to trust you with their journey until they feel heard and understood, first.

Throughout my experiences coaching parents of children with addictions, trusting solely in our perceptions and perspectives is a place where many of us end up getting lost or stuck. We know where they are, we know what they have experienced, and we know what they need to do to turn their life around. Unfortunately, our experiences are limited to our perspectives, what we have seen, felt and heard, without understanding exactly what they've experienced or felt. Our opinions and ideas come from a place of what we know and believe, not fully taking into consideration what we don't know or understand. Selfless listening provides a process for changing our perspectives and our ideas.

Mile 57

I started on my listening journey much by accident.

As a sales professional, the key component to my success was my ability to build lasting, trusting relationships. People trust me easily and engage me easily. I took pride in these abilities, to know people readily trusted me.

The reason for this was I would engage in conversations where I did all the listening, while asking timely engaging questions along the way.

My goal was always to help clients and prospects find what they were looking for. The more I listened, the more I learned. The more I learned, the more I was able to effectively uncover and identify what they were attempting to accomplish and help them solve for. I became quite effective at solving complex business issues through my listening behaviors.

A primary reason for being able to help them was my selfless listening process helped me uncover issues, challenges, and experiences which were necessary to address the issue, but were not readily shared with people who could not be trusted.

One day I started reflecting on the relationship I had with my son. I wasn't listening to him. I was shaming him and telling him. I wasn't listening to him or understanding him. I couldn't help because he didn't trust me with the truth of where he was and what he was really struggling with. He was protecting himself from me and holding back information which would assist me in loving, encouraging and supporting him.

I started listening. The more I listened, the more he shared.

The more he shared, the more I learned.

The more I learned, the better our relationship of trust and love healed and grew.

It didn't place me in a position to solve his substance abuse disorder issues. After all they were not my responsibility, nor had they ever been. But, it did allow us to safely share information which helped both of us better navigate the struggles associated with his substance use disorder. And, it healed our relationship.

Listening, selfless listening, is one of the more powerful behavioral shifts I made in relation to my son. This behavior has redefined so much of our respective journeys. I encourage all parents to learn to commit to this behavior of selfless listening. It is a game changer.

Mile 58

I didn't decide to go to recovery when I lost my job, lost my home, lost my kids, or went to jail and lost my freedom.

I made a decision to go to recovery when I was sitting on a hill and realized I needed to do this for me.

After a talk I had given at a treatment facility, I had a conversation with one of the counselors. This was the story he shared about what triggered his recovery. It was a story that resonated with me.

I told myself I would stop using heroin if I ever started injecting it. Then I told myself I would stop, if I lost my job and got kicked out of the house. Then I told myself, I would stop if I ever went to jail. Then, I found myself in jail. I had crossed every boundary I had established and I was still using. I stopped using and went to recovery after I got out of prison and relapsed. I decided I didn't want to do this anymore. - This conversation was taken from an interview I conducted with a young man who had completely turned his life around after years of heroin use. Even though he had anticipated what his "bottom" would be defined by, his addiction took him beyond it, until he decided it was time.

"Finding the bottom," is a popular term, often referenced in parent group interactions. It is more legend and myth than anything. Like many phrases in the addiction lexicon, "the bottom" is a tired phrase few people really comprehend.

For many, the "bottom" is a solitary, tragic event occurring in a person's life which causes them to finally decide or realize they need to change their life. Utilizing this loose buzzword descriptor, parents continually analyze each monumental event in their child's addiction-filled life in the hopes this last catastrophic event would finally be the one, their child's "bottom."

Overdose, severe illness, arrest, jail, prison, loss of children, homelessness, rape, a severe beating all are likely or potential "bottoms" to a reasonable person. Except "reasonable" or "normal" are unlikely the words one would use to describe the behaviors or the mindset of a person in active substance use.

A person in active addiction has likely experienced some or many of the life changing events previously identified. Despite those experiences, parents frustratingly discover their child rarely responds to them with a shift toward recovery. Instead, their child adapts to this new situation with the same old behaviors. Despite the patterns in these adaptive behaviors, with no change in sight, parents continue to hope for something to trigger them out of their substance use.

As parents, we experience wide ranging and bizarre behaviors or outcomes with our addicted children. We watch, we hope, we wait for that defining event to create an opportunity for us to swoop in and convince our child they can't get any lower, encouraging them to declare it their bottom and push for them to go to recovery. This has worked, although it is rarely successful in the long run. Many times, parents successfully leverage their child's low point effectively enough to get them to enter recovery, only to discover the heartbreaking news their child has left the treatment center after a few days and returned to the life they were living. This serves as a reminder, finding the bottom an elusive dream.

No one can predict or anticipate what event or situation becomes a call to action or their impetus for change, their commitment to recovery.

Every story is unique, and every motivational event toward recovery is quite personal. But there is a common thread to most of these incredible recovery stories...

"I knew I needed to do something."

As much as we would love to inspire, encourage, motivate, and guide our children to and through recovery, the fundamental driver for success and commitment is an individual one.

Parents, this is not your journey, your objectives, your decision, your timing, or your program.

The best you can offer in this process is to quit hovering, admonishing, challenging, telling, pushing, or engaging in relation to your child's recovery. Choosing to detox, go to rehab, and to work at their recovery is all driven by an individually driven motivational process. It is not your job to define their "bottom" or rescue them from it.

Mile 59

We assign far too much responsibility to ourselves for directing our children into recovery, take way too much credit when they do, and pin too much hope on the outcome.

When recovery and treatment fail, as sadly it often does, we are devastated because we convinced ourselves they were ready. This serves to remind parents that we only have control of so much. Sadly, parents put their lives on hold in anticipation of the day they go into recovery.

When it finally happens, they celebrate the day, only to crash into a broken, emotional heap with every post-treatment relapse. Each time exclaiming, "I thought they were ready."

I know you were ready for them to embrace their recovery; but, how well did you really understand their readiness and their commitment? Had they really experienced enough of a life in complete brokenness to follow through on their willingness to commit to embracing a new and different path? Or, did you show up and rescue them from the streets and their chaos in such a timely manner they were willing to *give it a try*? What was their commitment level?

Commitment is a powerful and telling word. It is one few of us understand and in a high state of hopefulness we readily embrace anything that looks like a commitment as true commitment. Unfortunately, many commitments are more readily defined as intention or desire. There is a quantum difference between intention, willingness, or desire and commitment. Simply going to treatment because it sounded like a good idea or I think I am ready, demonstrates about as much commitment as an individual tackling their annual New Year's Resolution. It is more like, I will give it a shot and see how it goes. Once it gets too hard, difficult, or challenging, or when it doesn't go the way I would have liked or preferred, the resolution goes out the window.

Commitment to recovery is a very personal, pivotal decision. It is least successful when done to please or satisfy someone else's desires or pleadings. It works when the person who walks into that treatment facility declares, "I am not living like this anymore" and doesn't negotiate how or when or where. Their recovery begins "now" because they decided it had to. And, they will do whatever is necessary to get there.

A very telling sign of this mindset is if they make this determination, this commitment and take this action without your involvement. This demonstrates they are doing it for themselves and recognize they need to own the actions and the process without enrolling or pleasing anyone else to make it happen.

We had tried for years to get my son to enter and complete a treatment program. Many times would begin one, but often dropped out after a few days. He was homeless this last time he went to treatment, this time completely on his own. It started with him going to detox, on his own. When he got out, he stopped by to let us know he would be entering a treatment program and not be concerned if we don't hear from him for a couple of weeks. After thirty days, he completed his first ever treatment program and found a sober living house to transition to. He did this all on his own. He kept us informed of his activities but didn't ask us for help along the way. Since then, he has been actively doing the ongoing work necessary to support his recovery. While this is my son's story, this is typical of someone who, after years of substance use disorder in their life, finally decided they had enough. Like my son, when they made that decision, they figured it out, often on their own.

If you are a parent or a loved one who is struggling to get someone to go to recovery, stop looking for their bottom, stop trying to chase after or convince them! When they are ready, they will take care of it.

Instead:

- Make a commitment to them, when they are ready to embrace a different path for their life, you will be there to support them (not help them) and walk with them (not for them) on this new path;
- Let them make the call. At some point, they will examine the contrast between the life they love, the life they have lost and the life they are living. When they decide, if they decide, the life they are living is unacceptable to them, they will make the move toward recovery because it is what they want and are committed to.

Mile 60

Your child's recovery is not your business! This is the major take-away from this book.

The more I learn about addiction, recovery, parenting and all the dynamics associated with the struggle, the stronger my commitment to this statement.

Your child's recovery is not your business, unless....

- You have been asked and encouraged *by your child* to be part of the process; <u>and</u>,
- You have made a *commitment to engage in your own recovery education program* involving:
    o Recognizing your own addictive behaviors and its toxic impact on your life and others.
    o Immersing yourself in addiction education – not just the behaviors, but the underlying issues.
    o Committing to a recovery education process which goes beyond teaching you how to respond to the behaviors of your addicted child as a form of self-protection education.
    o Understanding your child's addiction journey from their experiences, not yours.

I have been on my journey for nearly ten years. In the first two years, my focus was do whatever it took to get my son to embrace sustained recovery.

I protected him, coddled him, screamed at him, shamed him, hugged him, loved him and put my best inspirational talk before him.

Nothing worked. I was frustrated, upset, angry, disappointed and hurt – note, these are all toxic emotions which help no one!

Then, I went through a personal transformation period which became the foundation for the work through 100Pedals. I went through several incredible phases of personal and spiritual development. This educational and developmental work resulted in a much higher level of understanding of the issue of addiction, what I was dealing with, and what needed to occur for my son to embrace a sustained recovery.

After six years of work, nothing really changed, except me. All good, except my primary objective was still helping my son find and embrace his long-term recovery.

Finally, after eight total years on this journey, I made another monumental shift. I committed to unconditionally love my son, despite his addiction, regardless of his choices. I accepted the reality that his addiction was his journey, as was his long-term recovery. I made a commitment to love him and engage him whenever I could, wherever I could. At times it really hurt to experience him in his active addiction.

It still does.

Mile 61

In the process, something changed.

We talked, we laughed, and we shared. We enjoyed each other once again. *We were and are healing.* Today, he is working hard on his long-term recovery and he sometimes shares his lessons and his experiences in relation to this work. We talk sports, music, family, stories – *we are healing.*

It is my responsibility, it is my role, to make certain my son knows he is loved, he is valued, he is appreciated, he is amazing, and he is safe. When he knows he can trust me with who he is, where he is, I am being the dad he needs me to be, without criticism, judgment or condemnation.

I make our interactions about who he is, where he is and how much I love him right there, in that moment. These behaviors demonstrate how important our relationship is.

I can only be involved or included when and if he invites me.

And, when/if he does, I am better prepared and equipped to support him exactly in the way he needs. My confidence in this mindset comes from having done the hard work necessary in supporting him.

Lately, I have been studying a great deal of social media conversation about what qualifies as recovery from an addiction. There are a lot of passionate opinions about what is a very personal, individual process. As an individual in his own recovery from my issues with alcohol and the parent of a child dealing with a heroin addiction, I have direct experience with a variety of approaches and results.

Recovery, the outcome, the result, and the process are really a matter of personal choice. It cannot be governed by someone else's defined objectives and rules. There are several historically popular programs, methodologies, and processes each reporting varied, measurable successes. There are also other successful, innovative approaches and philosophies which are touted as controversial, risky or complex. Each of these programs can lay claim to their extensive and demonstrated successes and accomplishments. They all work and they all don't work. It does not make one right, or another wrong.

Defining the rules for someone else's recovery, does not honor or support the work an individual is engaged in to find their way out of their substance use disorder. Recovery is a complex, complicated process. As we learn more about substance use disorder and alternative treatment modalities, any limited willingness to accept or examine alternative treatment methods disrespects the research and the efforts of those who are working on their recovery in the best manner they know how.

If there was a one-size fits all methodology, the debate over which treatment programs work best, would be moot. Truth is that recovery is not an exact science and there are multiple roads to success and accomplishment; including how someone defines and achieves their long-term recovery.

Recovery is a complex, maddening and confusing process. It is filled with starts and stops, successes and failures, including many trials and errors. Some people's definition of recovery is to be completely substance free; while others are seeking to define recovery as finally breaking free of their drug of choice. It is complicated. And, the perfect answer is an illusive one.

Mile 62

Who am I to tell someone else how their recovery should be defined?

I know what works for me, why it works for me, and this is what I embrace. If someone wishes to know what I believe works best, I will be happy to share the experiences and joy in my process and approach, and why it worked for me. That is as far as I will go. I am not willing to define, judge, or critique someone else's definition of recovery, or the process they are using to get there. That part is personal.

I would, however, encourage every person who is battling an addiction, including loved ones who are battling the issues of co-dependency or enabling, to take time to define what your life in recovery looks like. Before tackling any program, you will need a clear vision of what you want your recovered life to be.

Work on creating that vision to the point where you can articulate an image of what recovery looks like in your life, including what is present and what is absent from your life.

Operating from a place of vision and clarity will put in you in a more empowered space to define your recovery program and what the process needs to be for you to find what you are looking for.

How you get to the desired outcome for your life is up to you. You can't know what path to take without a strong sense of what the finish line looks like. Make a commitment to the life you desire. Make a commitment to the program that you believe best drives you to that outcome.

Whatever program or outcome you embrace, the real work and the process is yours to own and not someone else's to approve of. It's your life, your recovery, your program, and your responsibility.

Make a commitment to the process, as well as the outcome.

Never give up on the mission, the vision, the objective. It is a focused commitment to the outcome which drives you to accomplishment, not embracing a program which meets someone else's definition of recovery.

Four guiding truths for parents in regard to personal recovery behaviors:

1. My child will have to work hard for their recovery. They don't need me to do any of the work or help lighten the load.

2. I will have to work hard for my recovery. If I haven't been working on it, this is where my focus needs to be.

3. Our two recovery programs are not related, connected, or interdependent. My recovery is dependent upon me learning:

   - What addiction is.
   - How addiction and substance use affects and influences my child.
   - How to be the parent my child needs me to be regardless of where they are on their addiction journey.

4. The better I get at creating a healthy separation from my child's addiction and recovery, the better equipped and prepared I am to love, support, encourage, and engage them regardless of where they are on their journey.

Mile 63

As I was putting this book together, I reflected on how far I had come in my recovery from my son's addiction.

I found myself celebrating the transformational experiences and the gifts they have been to both my son and I. If I had not done the hard work on myself, I am not certain my son and I would be experiencing a healing in our relationship.

There was a point in this journey where the only acceptable outcome for me was for him to find, embrace, and celebrate his extended recovery. The only way I could be at peace with my role as his dad and as a man in this world, was if somehow, I was able to help guide him to recovery from his addiction. Defining our relationship, or limiting the scope of our relationship to one single outcome, his recovery, put an extremely high burden on both of us. I had defined success and accomplishment as father and son by one outcome, recovery. And, without recovery, we could not celebrate who we are as father and son.

Think about living a life with this limiting objective in mind: *"Until my child finds and embraces long-term recovery, I cannot find peace in my life."*

Imagine the responsibility this statement assigns to my son. I was making him responsible for my joy. Not only was he responsible for finding joy in his life, but he was also being held accountable for mine. Assigning him this responsibility freed me of any obligation to grow or change. Instead, I put it all on him. Everything was dependent upon him embracing his long-term recovery. All he needed to do was to comply with my expectations and everything would be okay for all of us. What an unfair, tremendous burden to place on my child. Didn't he have enough to cope with already?

Sadly, this is how many parents live with a child with substance use disorder. They put their life on hold until their child embraces long-term recovery. The work, the burden, the responsibility for change is the child's. This is too much to put on a child and doesn't assign much responsibility for personal growth and development to the parent.

What happens to your life…

- If he never finds his recovery?
- If his current cycle of addiction, recovery, and relapse is as good as it gets?
- If nothing ever changed or improved from what it is today?
- If we never have a "normal" relationship?
- If we never get back what we have lost?
- If we cannot find that road to healing and recovery?
- Does this mean my life remains in this fixed, stuck position waiting for recovery to happen?

Is it possible for me to find peace and joy in my life despite the chaos which exists within it?

I am hoping your answer to the last question is "yes." Statistically, there is a strong possibility addiction will be a constant in your life. If that is the case, then what?

Mile 64

When confronted with addiction in your family, engaging in your own recovery process is critical for health and healing.

This involves learning to redefine your role and behavior as a parent of a child with an addiction. There are no guarantees that changing your attitude, behaviors, and actions will bring recovery to your child; but it most likely will bring progressive healing to a heart broken by a loved one's addiction. In my coaching interactions with parents, the common denominators among those who have found a healing peace is in their commitment to incremental personal change.

For those who are looking to break free from the grip of addiction, I can promise you your life will change, your relationship with your child will be different, and you can find peace in the chaos once you embrace your own recovery journey.

I have shifted into a space, over time and not perfectly, where these components are a key part of my interactions and behaviors. I know it works because I have experienced amazing personal healing and have witnessed a tremendous, profound shift toward a healthy relationship with my son even though his journey is still tumultuous.

Parents, we do not have the right to sit on the sidelines, judge the process, evaluate their progress, and define success and failure from our own narrow behavioral segments, without having gone through our own rigorous developmental learning process first. This is not fair to your child, your family, or yourself. Engaging from the sidelines short circuits a critical healing and educational phase which inhibits personal development, education, understanding and empathy. We can only be the recovery resource we desire to be with our child when we do our own work, when we understand how difficult and challenging this work is, and when we can get out of the way to allow others to do theirs. It is from that place in our own recovery where we will experience and appreciate our own personal journey and discover how to love and encourage those as they walk out theirs.

Mile 65

It is time for you to continue on your own path from here.

We have covered a lot of ground over the first sixty-five miles to get you moving along on your own personal and difficult journey. Remember, you are never alone. If you need some guidance and assistance to navigate your journey further, there are resources available, provided you reach out and ask.

As you continue from here, please remember the following:

1. Even in the most trying of times, find a way to keep moving forward. Try new activities, learn new pursuits, or sports, or travel. Find a physical way to move your body and your heart will follow.
2. Healthy meditative activities clear your head and recharge your spirit. Take the time to be quiet, still and unclutter your busy mind. Detach to be able to re-connect.
3. Trust in your love over everything. Remember, fear corrupts great ideas and options.
4. Practice love and acceptance. Meet your child where they are, for who they are.
5. Selfless listening heals broken relationships and helps broadens your perspective beyond what you know and believe.
6. Find someone you can trust with your journey and be authentically vulnerable with them.

7. Embrace the superior emotions of joy, love, peace, gentleness. They allow you to receive guidance and encouragement and wisdom.
8. Respond with purpose to difficult emotionally charged situations. Avoid reacting to them.
9. Live and celebrate the gift of what you have discovered about yourself and others on this journey. Do what you can to release the experience of what you believe or think you have lost.
10. Commit to and embrace your own recovery program. It is a gift to be celebrated and worth the effort.

Thank you for riding these miles with me. As you begin to complete the rest of your journey, please remember to embrace it for what it is, a learning adventure. If you get lost or isolated, reach out and ask for guidance.

Recommended reading

Beyond Addiction, Jeffrey Foote

Provides a fresh perspective for parents and loved ones to interact with someone with substance use disorder. This book offers an in-depth look at the Community Reinforcement and Family Training (CRAFT) approach which is a refreshing, effective alternative to standard "tough love" methods. A fundamental component in the CRAFT approach is discovering how effective communication techniques, particularly motivational interviewing, productive engages everyone into the recovery and treatment discussion.

Beyond the Yellow Brick Road, Bob Meehan

An excellent book for parents raising adolescent children. Provides parents with clear guidelines for setting and honoring rules and boundaries for both themselves and their children. This book is refreshingly direct while offering some very clear, concise perspectives on various drugs and substances and their addictive and behavioral impact on young, developing minds.

Positive Addiction, Willam Glasser

Presents an eye-opening, research-based summary of two behavioral mindsets: those who have lost hope and those who believe there is always an answer. It provides powerful insights into the psychology of a person who has lost hope, such as one who struggles with substance use disorder, and the challenges associated with shifting out of this mindset. The contrasting view, those who believe there is an answer, facilitates a better understanding of the incredibly and powerful differences between the two.

Overcoming Opioid Addiction, Adam Bisaga

This book provides research-based medical treatment perspectives to substance use disorder. This is the most recent publication on this list and is highly recommended for parents and family members with a loved one with substance use disorder. Offers accurate and timely information on medically assisted treatment, harm reduction, family support behaviors, and more; plus a check-list for identifying the best treatment facility for a loved one.

Unbroken Brain, Maia Szalavitz

This book offers an in-depth understanding to the impact of different substances on the individual, both physically and psychologically, while providing this viewpoint from the perspective of the user, in both active use and recovery. It also provides an excellent perspective on the influences trauma and pre-existing psychological conditions have on addiction. Finally, it demonstrates and supports many of the treatment methodologies identified in "Overcoming Opioid Addiction."

About Dave Cooke

Dave Cooke is a popular blogger, author, professional speaker, and parent. Having spent much of his professional career as a strategist, personal development professional and executive coach, Dave has committed his life to following the powerful, challenging passion – being an inspirational and educational resource to parents dealing with addiction related issues in their families. Dave continues to be grateful for the lessons he continues to learn on his addiction education journey.

The 100Pedals organization provides parents and loved ones with educational programs and support resources to help them navigate the chaos of substance use disorder in their family. These include addiction education seminars and workshops, group and individual coaching programs, and other resources to:

- *Provide deep insights to complex issues of substance use disorder*
- *Emphasize the perspectives and experiences of the person with the addiction*
- *Teach participants to meet and engage their loved one wherever they are*
- *Provide tools for interacting without judgment, criticism or condemnation*
- *Help parents discover how to be the parent their child needs them to be*
- *Learn how to release feelings of guilt, fear, shame*

Parents, loved ones, and other family members can find all these resources at www.100Pedals.com.